D1602262

Twayne's United States Authors Series

Sylvia E. Bowman, *Editor*

INDIANA UNIVERSITY

Melvin B. Tolson

MELVIN B. TOLSON

By JOY FLASCH

Langston University

 215

Twayne Publishers, Inc.   ::   New York

To my husband, Harold,
and my children—Chris, Julie, and Jeanine

Preface

During his sixty-six years, Melvin Beaunorus Tolson, an outstanding black poet, produced only three books of poetry which were published; but he is recognized today as a unique and challenging poet by those acquainted with his work. An artist who espoused a difficult poetic style at a time when such a style was not the "fashion," particularly for a black poet, he was willing to sacrifice popularity during his lifetime and trust the "vertical audience" of the future to recognize the true value of his work.

Tolson was an unusual man as well as an unusual poet. He cared for people intensely. His students, colleagues, old friends, passing acquaintances—both the individual and the masses, the black and the white—were aware of his personal concern for them. He inspired devotion bordering on adulation in many who knew him well. In the 1970 spring commencement address at Langston University, Langston, Oklahoma, where Tolson had taught for almost twenty years, James Farmer, a former student of his at Wiley College in Marshall, Texas, and one of the founders of CORE and former assistant secretary of education, health and welfare, stated: "M. B. Tolson, one of the greatest black poets America has produced, was a genius. . . . He taught me everything I know and many things which I have forgotten."

There are those, of course, who cannot comfortably read Tolson's vivid descriptions of the accomplishments of the black man, despite centuries of atrocities and humiliations inflicted upon him by the "Great White World." In like manner, his work is not popular either with those black Americans who recognize themselves in his picture of the hypocritical "Black Bourgeoisie" because of their materialistic, white middle-class values or with those proponents of the "Black Esthetic" who resent his addressing his poetry to all who will read and appreciate it rather than his restricting his audience to black readers.

Tolson had courage. Unable to abide fence straddlers, neither could he side with extremists whose views he found simplistic. As a black poet, he wrote with pride about his people—their past, present, and future—but his standards and integrity as an artist required freedom so that his poetic style could flower in the manner which would permit fullest development. The resulting intellectual, allusive, philosophical style addresses itself to all who recognize the wit, the humor, the satire, the memorable characters, the metaphors, and the sheer poetry of his work. Ever mindful of his heritage and of his responsibility as a black poet, he nevertheless made clear the necessity of the artist to develop without limitations of any kind on his artistic imagination.

This volume, the first book-length study of Tolson, serves as an introduction to him and his works. Chapter 1, a brief biography, makes clear his long apprenticeship and dedication to the Muse. It not only discusses his published works but also describes briefly his unpublished manuscripts: a book of poems entitled "A Gallery of Harlem Portraits" (1932); three novels—"Beyond the Zaretto" (1924), "The Lion and the Jackal" (1939), and "All Aboard" (1952); and mentions several of his unpublished plays, including two full-length dramas—"The Moses of Beale Street" and "Southern Front." In addition, Tolson wrote many one-act plays, such as "The House By the Side of the Tracks," "The ABC Café on Deep Eighteenth," and "Bivouac on the Santa Fe." He also dramatized Walter White's *The Fire in the Flint* and George Schuyler's *Black No More*. During the Depression years, Tolson wrote a column for the Washington *Tribune* entitled "Cabbages and Caviar." Though the settings for his works are as varied as Oklahoma and Africa, his subject in almost every poem, play, essay, and novel he wrote is the black man.

Besides these unheralded works, Tolson produced three books of poetry: *Rendezvous with America* (1944), *Libretto for the Republic of Liberia* (1953), and *Harlem Gallery: Book I, The Curator* (1965). These published works, highly regarded by most of his critics, are analyzed in detail in chapters 2, 3, and 4. Chapter 5 provides a comparison of Tolson's development with that of some of his contemporaries and an assessment of his contribution to twentieth-century literature. Actually, his poetry has received comparatively little attention from many literary critics. My hope, as one who was privileged to be Professor Tolson's

Preface

colleague and friend during the last years of his life and as one who has much respect and admiration for his contribution to American literature, is that this introductory work will attract critics and readers as yet unaware of the complexity and worth of his poetry to the exciting challenge which awaits those who would plumb its depths in full exploration.

JOY FLASCH

Langston University
Langston, Oklahoma
January 1, 1972

Acknowledgments

For a Title III grant which enabled me to complete my doctoral course work and thesis out of which this study grew, I am indebted to the Langston University administrative personnel who recommended me: Dr. William H. Hale, former President; Dr. Larzette G. Hale, former Director of Development; Dr. William E. Sims, President and former Dean of Academic Affairs; and Dr. Elwyn E. Breaux, Chairman of the Department of English and Foreign Languages.

I am deeply grateful to Dr. Samuel B. Woods, Jr., Professor of English, Oklahoma State University, who helped me shape and focus my materials and who assisted me in establishing a basis for the criticism and evaluation of Tolson's work. Dr. Clinton Keeler, Chairman of the English Department, Oklahoma State University, and Dr. D. Judson Milburn, Professor of English, Oklahoma State University, gave me several helpful suggestions; and Mr. Laron Clark, former Director of Development and Librarian, Langston University, assisted me in locating materials.

Had Melvin B. Tolson not encouraged me to begin this work, I would never have had the confidence to attempt it. Mrs. Ruth Tolson made her husband's unpublished notes and papers available to me after his death in August, 1966; and she also spent many hours giving me biographical data and assisting me in finding information. Ruth Marie Tolson, a member of the library staff at Howard University, Washington, D.C., filed her father's papers and aided me in finding specific materials. Dr. Melvin B. Tolson, Jr., Professor of Modern Languages, University of Oklahoma, gave me biographical information, read my manuscript, and assisted me in interpreting various passages in his father's work. Another son, Dr. Arthur L. Tolson, Professor of Black History at Southern University, Baton Rouge, Louisiana, and author of *The Black Oklahomans, A History: 1541–1972*, has written letters of encouragement since I began working on this book. Mrs. Helen Tolson Wilson, sister of the poet, gave me biographical information about the poet's family and early life. Without the assistance and encouragement of the Tolsons, this work would not have been possible.

I am also grateful to my colleagues, friends, parents, and other members of my family who have had faith in me, especially my husband, Harold, who shares my warm regard for Professor Tolson and his work and who has given me his active support from beginning to end.

For permission to quote from copyrighted material, acknowledgment is made to the following: Dodd, Mead and Company, Inc., for poems from *Rendezvous with America* (1944); Twayne Publishers, Inc., for excerpts from *Libretto for the Republic of Liberia* (1953) and *Harlem Gallery: Book I, The Curator* (1965).

Contents

Chronology

1900 Melvin Beaunorus Tolson born February 6 in Moberly, Missouri, to the Reverend Mr. Alonzo Tolson and Lera Hurt Tolson.

1900 Lived in Moberly, New Franklin, Rolla, DeSota, and Slater, Missouri.

1912 Lived in Oskaloosa, Iowa. First poem published in the "Poet's Corner" of the Oskaloosa newspaper.

1913 Lived in Mason City, Iowa; Independence, Kansas; Kansas City, Missouri.

1915 Class poet; director and actor in Greek Club's Little Theatre; captain of football team, Lincoln High School, Kansas City, Missouri.

1918 Graduated from Lincoln High School; worked in a packing house.

1919 Enrolled in Fisk University, Nashville, Tennessee.

1920 Enrolled in Lincoln University, Oxford, Pennsylvania; won awards in speech, debate, dramatics, and Classical literatures; captain of football team.

1922 Married Ruth Southall of Virginia on January 29.

1923 Graduated from Lincoln University with honors in June.

1924 Accepted position as instructor of English and speech at Wiley College, Marshall, Texas; continued writing poetry; wrote novel (unpublished), "Beyond the Zaretto."

1929 Coached Wiley College debate teams, which established ten-year winning streak; wrote poems, plays, short stories, novels.

1930 Worked on master's degree in Department of English and Comparative Literature at Columbia University; met V. F. Calverton, editor of *Modern Quarterly;* wrote "Cabbages and Caviar" column for Washington *Tribune;* organized sharecroppers in South Texas.

1932   Completed 340-page book of poetry, "A Gallery of Harlem Portraits"; book rejected by publishers; did not write for several years.

1935   Wiley College debate team coached by Tolson defeated national champions, University of Southern California, before eleven hundred people.

1939   Completed novel (unpublished), "The Lion and the Jackal." Poem "Dark Symphony" won first place in National Poetry Contest sponsored by American Negro Exposition in Chicago. V. F. Calverton, best friend, died of leukemia.

1941   "Dark Symphony" published in *Atlantic Monthly.*

1944   *Rendezvous with America,* book of collected poems, published by Dodd, Mead and Company, Inc.

1945   Won Omega Psi Phi Award for Creative Literature.

1947   Appointed poet laureate of Liberia by President V. S. Tubman in January; left Wiley College to become professor of English and drama at Langston University, Langston, Oklahoma.

1951   Received *Poetry* magazine's Bess Hokim Award for long psychological poem, "E. & O.E."

1952   Langston University Dust Bowl Players, directed by Tolson, staged adaptation of Walter White's *The Fire in the Flint* in Oklahoma City for National Association for the Advancement of Colored People meeting; completed novel (unpublished), "All Aboard"; dramatized G. Schuyler's *Black No More.*

1953   *Libretto for the Republic of Liberia* published by Twayne Publishers, Inc.

1954   Awarded honorary degree, Doctor of Letters, by Lincoln University, Oxford, Pennsylvania; honored at literary tea, Liberian Embassy, Washington, D.C.; admitted to Knighthood of the Order of the Star of Africa, an honor conferred by Ambassador Simpson of Liberia; elected mayor of Langston (reelected three times); became permanent Bread Loaf Fellow in poetry and drama.

1956   Attended inauguration of President Tubman in Liberia.

1964   Underwent major surgery for abdominal cancer in April and December.

1965   Received national and international attention as result of Karl Shapiro's prepublication review of *Harlem Gallery:*

    Book I, The Curator published by Twayne Publishers, Inc.; presented copy of book to presidential party in White House; retired as professor of English and drama at Langston University; awarded honorary degree, Doctor of Humane Letters, Lincoln University, Oxford, Pennsylvania; elected to New York *Herald Tribune* book review board; given District of Columbia Citation and Award for Cultural Achievement in Fine Arts; became first appointee to the Avalon Chair in Humanities at Tuskegee Institute; spoke at Library of Congress under auspices of Gertrude Clarke Whittall Poetry and Literature Fund; underwent third operation for cancer in October.

1966   Received annual poetry award of American Academy of Arts and Letters, a grant ($2,500) on May 25; entered St. Paul's Hospital, Dallas, Texas, in June, where three operations were performed in a three-month period; died August 29; buried in Summit View Cemetery, Guthrie, Oklahoma, September 3.

CHAPTER *1*

Melvin Tolson: Poet, Teacher, Philosopher

> A champion of the People versus Kings—
> His only martyrdom is poetry;
> A hater of the hierarchy of things—
> Freedom's need is his necessity.
> —Tolson, "The Poet"

SMALL, gray-haired, brown-skinned Professor Melvin Tolson slowly climbed the curved marble staircase of the White House. He paused to rest a moment and shook his head in disbelief. Glancing back at the group of friends and relatives at his heels, he smiled and then sang softly to himself as he made his way up the stairs: "We are climbing Jacob's ladder." [1] Only three months before he had undergone his second major abdominal operation for cancer in less than a year, but this climb was one he savored. Now, in 1965 at the age of sixty-five, he was at the White House to present a copy of his latest book of poetry, *Harlem Gallery: Book I, The Curator,* to the President of the United States. It seemed impossible that a few weeks before he had almost despaired that he would ever live to see his book in print or to complete the final year of his forty-three years of college teaching and have time at last to write during the daylight hours.

As the entourage moved down the hall, Tolson spied the name of Hobart Taylor on a door. Again he had the feeling that he would wake up momentarily. He knew that Hobart Taylor, the former classmate of his oldest son, was a member of the White House staff. But even more vivid was his recollection of walking past the White House in his own youth when the only black men to be seen there wore white coats and were either coming out or going in. It was true that he knew no one else there except Zephyr, one of President Johnson's cooks who had been his student years before; but most of his ex-students—James Farmer was his favorite illustration—had long since bypassed the kitchen for the upper echelons of government or other service.

As the Tolson party neared the anteroom where he was to autograph copies of the recently published *Harlem Gallery* for the presidential party and for his own proud group, Tolson thought back to the beginning of his odyssey—to the chain of circumstances leading to his taking the road less traveled by, the road which had led to his being invited to the White House this morning of March 29, 1965.

I *Genesis in Missouri*

Melvin Beaunorus Tolson, who was born February 6, 1900, in Moberly, Missouri, was the oldest son of the Reverend Mr. Alonzo Tolson, an itinerant minister in the Methodist Episcopal Church. Of Negro, Indian, and Irish descent, Melvin's father had only an eighth-grade education; but he took a number of correspondence courses and taught himself Latin, Hebrew, and Greek. He had little faith in college degrees, and he wanted Melvin to become a minister in the tradition of his father, grandfather, and great-grandfather; instead, his son earned two college degrees and was awarded two honorary doctorates, spent almost half a century as a college teacher, and produced four offspring who collected a total of twelve college degrees.

Young Melvin's family moved frequently from town to town in Missouri and Iowa. His father was a good provider who gardened, kept the cellar full, and was handy around the house. He enjoyed hunting, but one day when his four small children were standing in front of him, stairstep fashion, watching him clean his gun, it suddenly discharged and a bullet whizzed directly over their heads. He never hunted again. An aristocratic-looking man with a straight carriage, the quiet-spoken minister, who was also an active member of the Republican party, spent forty-five years in the ministry and died in 1949 at the age of seventy.

Tolson's mother was a Cherokee Indian whose father had been killed when he had refused to permit himself to become enslaved. An excellent seamstress, she helped bolster the family income by sewing. Lera Tolson sang beautifully, and the Tolsons had their own family ensemble: Melvin played the mandolin; Yutha, the violin; Helen, the piano; Rupert, the drums; and they all sang.

Helen took voice, piano, and dancing lessons and later attended a conservatory of music in Kansas City. Though Tolson could not be considered a musician, he loved music and had a keen ear for it.

Alonzo and Lera Tolson had a harmonious marriage. The children never heard their parents argue; and, when the children misbehaved, the parents talked to them or deprived them of their privileges but seldom spanked them. Because they were the minister's children, they were not encouraged to mingle much with other children, but they enjoyed playing ball and sleigh riding together.[2] Melvin, who was studious as a child, planned to be a physician; and he occasionally prepared weeds as medicine for his younger sisters and brother. Although small, he was a healthy, muscular, athletic child. One day after he had been slugged by an Irish boy on an opposing ward-school football team, he complained to his tackle, another Irish boy, Al. Al promised, "The next time that S.O.B. comes around I'll get him." But Melvin got him first. Then a black player on the other team knocked Melvin down, and the free-for-all began. They were a bunch of poor Irish, Afro-American, Swedish, and Jewish boys whose only barrier was social, Tolson recalled, not racial. He reflected that this interpretation of the social environment—social barriers, not racial—stayed with him throughout his life.

Those boyhood days in Missouri were captured in part by the poet in one of the many notebooks that he kept and in which he reminisced about his and his family's colorful past:

> . . . my little walnut-hued mother . . . was a descendant from antebellum fugitives who hid themselves on the islands in the Mark Twain country and in the glooms of the Ozarks, from which they raided at midnight the slave plantations along the Missouri and the Mississippi. Out of the melting-pot of this clan came gun-toting preachers and hallelujahing badmen whose legends grew whiskers in the dead yellow hills. One, a giant riverman, stole the sheriff's white horse and rode it out of town to join Jesse James at Independence; another, unfrocked, blew the lock off the church door, defied the Law, and preached the Gospel of Jesus Christ, with his Forty-five on one side of the pulpit and his open Bible on the other.
>
> Of Irish, French, Indian, and African bloods the members of the clan gathered on New Year's Eve, the Christians sipping eggnog,

the sinners guzzling hard liquor. The young listened, wild-eyed and hush-mouthed, as elders spun Homeric tales, dipped snuff, smoked clay pipes, and belly-laughed at inferiors, white and black. . . .[3]

By the time Tolson was ten years old, he painted pictures, which he framed and peddled, and he and a friend, Claude, had their own tent show. Claude versified and invented mechanical toys, while Tolson painted the scenery and played Caesar. One day when he was painting a picture in his front yard, he sensed someone behind him. He turned and saw there a man who looked like the very artists he had seen in art books. The stranger, who was a passenger on a nearby train which had stopped because of a hot box, exclaimed in "Frenchified English, with a grandiloquent flourish: 'Marvelous! Marvelous! You must go to Paris with me! Where is your father?'" At last Melvin's dreams had come true, and he raced into the house to blurt out the good news to his mother. She parted the curtains, glared at the "bizarre figure" outside, and locked every door in the house.[4] Tolson never painted again; instead, he turned to poetry. Years later, however, his musical and artistic talents were revealed in his emphasis on sound, sight, and sense in his poetry—what he referred to as his "three S's of Parnassus."

About the time that Tolson was discovering the arts, he became acquainted with Mrs. George Markwell, a white lady who made her library available to the youngster who read everything to which he had access. In her home he had his first experience with racial prejudice when Mrs. Markwell's daughter told him one day that "The only Negro of worth is Booker T. Washington, and the only reason he has excelled is that he is half white. He would have been greater had he been all white." When Melvin asked her mother if this statement were true, Mrs. Markwell did not reply; instead, she sent him to the bookshelf for a copy of Thomas Carlyle's *French Revolution* and told him to look through the illustrations until he found the answer for himself. As he scanned the pages, he came to a picture of a magnificent white stallion on which was mounted a jet-black man resplendent in uniform—Touissant L'Ouverture. He never forgot this lesson, and in the years ahead racial pride became one of the chief themes of his conversation, lectures, and poetry.

II   *Encounter with Muse in Iowa*

Tolson had few experiences, however, with racial prejudice in his childhood; and he continued to be an avid reader as his family moved from Moberly to New Franklin to DeSota to Slater, Missouri, and then to Iowa. For several years he had been acquainted with Plato and Aristotle, whom his father discussed with him on afternoons when they went fishing together. Of his parents' influence on his writing, he said, "My mother was always making up verses in her head. She was highly intelligent and imaginative, but had little formal education. Like my father I was a bookworm. Later, much later, I began scribbling verses on tablets and scraps of paper. I repeated, over and over, Shakespeare's immortal words in Sonnet 50: 'Not marble, nor the gilded monuments/Of princes, shall outlive this powerful rhyme.' So at twelve, I decided to join the immortal poets in a future Paradise." [5]

His first published poem appeared in the "Poet's Corner" of an Oskaloosa newspaper in 1912. During his lectures on poetry years later, his eyes would twinkle as he told his audiences that he was inspired to be a poet as a child while he was reading verses on the tombstones in a local cemetery. One inscription read, "I am dead as all can see;/Prepare ye all to follow me." As he pondered this advice, two lines suddenly came to him: "To follow you I'm not content/Until I know which way you went." When he expounded seriously on inspiration, he paraphrased Thomas Edison's formula for invention by saying that poetry is one percent inspiration and 99 percent perspiration.

Tolson's family moved from Oskaloosa to Mason City, Iowa, and here Tolson "learned all he knew" about public speaking from his eighth-grade teacher, who was white and who trained him to be a perfectionist by having him say one poem over and over and by snapping her fingers to indicate when a word should be accented. He said that he could not help feeling slightly superior standing in front of the predominantly white audiences, his reddish-brown hair parted in the middle and slicked down with lard, as he recited the poems of one of the first black poets to gain national recognition, Paul Laurence Dunbar. Tolson tried at this time to imitate the dialect poems of Dunbar, and he little thought that his poetry would someday be compared not so much to that of Dunbar and other black poets as to that of T. S. Eliot, Ezra Pound, and Hart Crane.

Tolson attended high school in Kansas City, Missouri, where he was captain of the football team, class poet, and both director and actor in the Greek Club's Little Theatre. He worked in a packing house there for a while and then enrolled in 1919 in Fisk University in Nashville, Tennessee, for his freshman year in college.

III   *From College Student to College Instructor*

In 1920, Tolson enrolled in Lincoln University in Oxford, Pennsylvania, the oldest institution of higher education for black students in the United States. Founded as Ashmun Institute by Abolitionists before the Civil War, it was originally named for Jehudi Ashmun, the white founder of the Republic of Liberia. When Tolson lived in Ashmun Hall as a student at Lincoln, he little dreamed that twenty-seven years later he would be appointed poet laureate of Liberia. At Lincoln University he won awards in speech, debate, dramatics, and Classical literatures; and once more he was captain of the football team. "Cap," as he was called by his classmates, further juxtaposed his activities by writing poetry, by waiting tables along the famous Atlantic City boardwalk, and by teaching a course of freshman English when he was only a junior.

In Tolson's senior year at Lincoln University, he attended an Omega Psi Phi fraternity dance at which he noticed an attractive, red-haired girl talking with some friends. He pointed her out to a fraternity brother, who promptly bet him a dollar that she would not dance with him. Tolson put up his dollar, invited the young lady to dance, and in the process learned that she was Miss Ruth Southall from Virginia and that she was visiting relatives in Pennsylvania. When he went to collect his dollar, his friend paid him and then bet him another dollar that the visitor would not dance with him a second time. Tolson not only collected his second dollar but continued to dance with Miss Southall and capped the evening by escorting her home. She informed him afterwards, however, that his personality and intellect had impressed her more than his dancing ability.[6]

When, a year or so later, Ruth Southall agreed to marry Melvin

Tolson, she assumed the difficult but rewarding role of devoting her next forty-four years to a man with boundless energy and ambition—a radical, courageous, talented man who refused to act as a black man was supposed to act in the south Texas town of Marshall where they established a home. During their twenty-four-year stay in Marshall, she bore him four children: Melvin Beaunorus, Jr.; Arthur Lincoln; Wiley Wilson; and Ruth Marie. During this period, Tolson distinguished himself as a college teacher, speaker, debate coach, director of plays, and poet.

It was as a debate coach that the Tolson name first became known throughout the South and Southwest, for his Wiley College teams had at one time a ten-year winning streak. His formula for success was simple: (1) his debaters learned the logical fallacies; (2) they debated with their coach for one year before they could make the team. Melvin, Jr., frequently fell asleep in the living room to the drone of the debaters' voices, for the practice sessions did not begin until around nine o'clock in the evening. Often, when he awakened, startled, at two or three o'clock in the morning, the loud, heated voices made him fear that a fight was about to erupt.[7]

Those Wiley teams had everything, Tolson declared: reasoning, wit, satire, eloquence; and one of his teams was the first black debate team to be mentioned in the *International Journal of Forensics*. His debate team participated in the first interracial debate, which took place in Avery Chapel, Oklahoma City, in 1929, between Wiley College and Oklahoma City University; and other teams of his staged the first interracial debates in the South, Southwest, and on the East Coast. In a nondecision bout, a Wiley College team debated the University of Kansas when its team included the champion extemporaneous speaker of the United States. During the 1934–35 season, Tolson and his team traveled to the University of Southern California, where they debated the national champions. Before the debate, Tolson scouted the speech department, which was as large as all of Wiley College. When his team wanted to visit the campus, Tolson told his students, "Oh, they're not so much. We'll visit them after we win the debate just to show them we're good sports." [8] Confident of their coach's evaluation, his students proceeded to defeat the national champions before a crowd of eleven hundred people. When Mae West heard about the amazing record of the little Texas team, she asked to meet it, and for years Tolson proudly displayed the autographed picture she gave him.

Among Tolson's Wiley College debaters were Thomas Cole, the first black student to receive a doctorate from the University of Texas (he later became president of Wiley College); Frederick Douglass Weaver, grandson of the famous Frederick Douglass and later a member of the New York Public Housing Authority; and James Farmer, former assistant secretary of health, education and welfare. One of his outstanding debaters was a young man named Henry Heights, whose name Tolson used in *Harlem Gallery* as Hideho Heights ("Hideho" was derived from Cab Calloway's "Hi-de-ho!").

Tolson and his debaters had many encounters with racial prejudice as they traveled around the country. On one trip through the South, Tolson, Heights, and the other debaters stopped at a cafe; and when some white men came in, looked around suspiciously, and spoke in low but audible tones of "rape" and "catching them," Tolson and his students quickly lost their appetites. This place was one where they did not care to have their championship style of argumentation put to a test. On another trip when they stopped at a service station to buy gas, they asked to use the rest room, only to make a hasty departure when the owner appeared with his shotgun and fired a warning shot after their car as they drove away. Mrs. Tolson did not know about such adventures until years later, when she overheard her husband and his former students talking about the "good old days."

In 1938, near the end of Tolson's decade of debating trips, he received word that his mother had died, in her fifties, of cancer. She had always had a morbid fear of this disease, and during the next twenty-eight years, the dread affliction claimed three of her four children. She and Melvin had always been quite close; and, when his first book of poetry was published six years later, he wrote the following dedication: "To my Father, Alonzo, and The Memory of My Mother, Lera, *whose life was a greater poem than any I may write.*"

Near the end of the 1930's Tolson felt that interest in debate was waning, and he began to put more emphasis on drama. In his work as director of dramatic productions at Wiley College, he discovered several actors, directors, and other public figures in the making: Virgil Richardson, star of *The Big White Fog* (said by Broadway producer Abram Hill to have the best voice in America); Louise Pollard, featured in the Hollywood production of *The Lost City;* Lonnie Jackson, Broadway actor; Dorothea Towles, Dior model in Paris, and James Farmer.

Tolson had been writing all along, although teaching full time, coaching the debate team, and directing plays took most of his time. During these busy years and the ones following, he jotted down hundreds of ideas and outlines for poems, novels, and plays which he planned to write when he had the time. Some of the short plays which he completed were entitled "The House by the Side of the Tracks," "The ABC Cafe on Deep Eighteenth," "An Act of God," And "Upper Boulders in the Sun." One play, "Transfiguration Springs," revolves around a native white Virginian on an Oklahoma ranch who refuses the offer of his black neighbor to share his water supply during a drought. Rather than accept a favor from a black man, he steals his water, and his attitude changes only when his neighbor rescues the white man's wife from a dangerous situation. "Bivouac on the Santa Fe" pictures a small detachment of soldiers during the days of early Oklahoma statehood and sets up a three-way racial feud among a white man, a black man, and an Indian, the intensity of which is matched by a tornado, which forces the men either to help one another or to be destroyed.

Some of Tolson's full-length plays include "The Moses of Beale Street" and "Southern Front," both of which concern racial situations. In the 1950's while he was teaching at Langston University in north central Oklahoma, Tolson also adapted and dramatized George Schuyler's novel *Black No More* and Walter White's *The Fire in the Flint.* He staged the latter in 1952 at a meeting of the National Association for the Advancement of Colored People at Convention Hall in Oklahoma City for over five thousand people.

As early as 1924 he tried his hand at a novel, which he tentatively entitled "Beyond the Zaretto." The setting was on the Zaretto River in Africa. Another novel, written in 1935, was set in Ethiopia and was entitled "The Lion and the Jackal." He wrote a third novel, "All Aboard," during the 1950's while he was working on *Libretto for the Republic of Liberia* and finishing his dramatization of *Black No More.* At this time, Tolson felt that he achieved the best results when writing both prose and poetry, "one stimulating the other, one recuperating me for the other." He described his current novel in this way:

> "All Aboard" deals with that American institution and legend, the Pullman porter. It covers the period between the two World Wars. It grows out of intimate personal experience and research. The data in the Schomberg Collection of the Harlem Library were placed at the disposal of the writer by Dr. Lawrence D. Reddick, the curator. It is the odyssey of Duke Hands and the story of the unionization of the Pullman porters. It introduces a new literary device in which interior dialog (stream of consciousness) becomes exterior. . . . The characters, white and colored, in their interrelations, should give the work social as well as artistic significance.[9]

During this same period, Tolson was also experimenting with poetry of various types. His method was to imitate the masters, learning the rules for the various forms through using them. The content of his work arose, for the most part, from his own experiences; and his subject was the black man.

Tolson eventually completed his course work for a master of arts degree in English and comparative literature at Columbia University. By the fall of 1931, he had written his thesis except for the bibliography; but his work with the college debate teams and his creative writing took so much of his time during the 1930's that it was not until 1940 that he finally completed all the requirements for the degree. His objectives in his thesis, "The Harlem Group of Negro Writers," were threefold: (1) to give the social background of the Harlem Renaissance and the various sources in the black metropolis which caused the artistic and literary development of the "New Negro"; (2) to emphasize the lives and works of leading contemporary black essayists, short-story writers, novelists, and poets in the light of modern criticism; and (3) to interpret the attitudes and stylistic methods discovered in the Harlem Renaissance.

Chapter 1 of his thesis presents a perspective of Harlem—its history and recent vogues. Chapter 2, "The Negro or Harlem Renaissance," characterizes the movement, analyzes the influences of World War I and of white patrons on black artists, describes the work of the National Association for the Advancement of Colored People there, and surveys researches in Negro history. The remaining eleven chapters are devoted to individual black authors and their works: Countee Cullen, Langston Hughes, Claude Mc-Kay, Walter White, Eric Walrond, Rudolph Fisher, Jessie Fauset, George Schuyler, W. E. B. DuBois, James Weldon Johnson, and Wallace Thurman. Tolson referred often to these writers in his teaching, in his lectures around the country, and in his poetry. He dramatized plays by White and Schuyler several years later, as has been mentioned. In the introduction, he gives credit to the following persons for their suggestions: Rudolph Fisher, Wallace Thurman, Langston Hughes, Miss Zona Gale, Miss Harriet Monroe, Charles S. Johnson, and Arthur Christy.

Tolson's career as a writer received fresh impetus when he became acquainted with a young writer and editor, V. F. Calverton, through one of the many quirks of fate which, Tolson felt, marked his life. One morning during the 1930's Tolson and a Wiley mathematics teacher who was a novice short-story writer strolled to the corner drugstore in Marshall and purchased a copy of *The Modern Quarterly*. After they read that the editor, V. F. Calverton, had edited an anthology of black literature, Tolson sent Calverton some of his poems; and he soon received a letter which commended his vigor and inspiration and predicted that he might well become the next great poet. When they met, Calverton repeated his belief in Tolson's potential; and Tolson said, "You flatter me." Calverton looked at him a long moment, then said, "Why in hell should *I* flatter *you?*" [10] This meeting was the unusual beginning of a close friendship. Throughout his life, Tolson referred to Calverton as "the best friend I ever had." Both young men had intellectual interests; and, when Tolson was in New York, he had a key to the home of Calverton, who delighted in taking him, as Tolson phrased it, "places no Negro had ever been." Tolson told one of his speech classes at Langston University about a young white professor, who, at a party one evening, deliberately tried to bait him, but Tolson turned each of his pointed remarks aside pleasantly. Finally the professor said, "Tolson, you just can't be insulted, can you?" The poet smiled, "No, my friend. You see a less intelligent man than I can't insult me, and a more intelligent one won't."

Calverton introduced Tolson to numerous artists and writers in Greenwich Village, and he listened to and participated in all-night discussions which he said caused him to question almost everything in which he had ever believed, as the discussions ranged from art to God and back again. The experience was invaluable to him as a writer, and he found it difficult to return to the literary desert of southern Texas. When he did, he invited Calverton to come to Marshall to talk to his students. Calverton accepted, and Tolson recalled that it took a wagon and team to carry away the whiskey bottles afterward, but the students enjoyed an "intellectual banquet" such as they had never known before.

About this time, Tolson completed a three-hundred-and-forty-page book of poetry entitled "A Gallery of Harlem Portraits." Calverton encouraged him to send the manuscript in 1939 to Maxwell Perkins and Bennett Cerf. Cerf wrote that he had to reject it, not because of its lack of artistic merit, but because he thought it would not sell. Maxwell Perkins of Charles Scribner's Sons wrote Tolson sometime after he had also rejected the manuscript to express his regret: "I know that it is bitterly discouraging to try to find a publisher for anything much out of the ordinary, and for poetry of any kind perhaps. I wish we could have done the Portraits, but anybody who was in a publishing house and remembered the efforts that had been made in past years with poetical writings of talent and the large lack of success would understand also the publisher's difficulty." [11] The poet's reaction to these rejections was to put his "man-wrecked" manuscript in a trunk and not to write for several years.

IV *"Dark Symphony" Brings Tolson*
First National Attention as Poet

The incentive for renewing his efforts was an invitation from Marshall Davis, chairman of the judging board of the National Poetry Contest sponsored by the American Negro Exposition in Chicago in 1940. Besides Davis, Langston Hughes and Arna Bontemps served as judges. Tolson decided to enter—should he win, he would enjoy a trip to Chicago; and the result of his decision was "Dark Symphony," which won first place and was exhibited in the Hall of Literature in Chicago. Published in the *Atlantic Monthly,* the poem brought him national attention for the first time as a poet. One of the most popular of all Tolson's poems,[12] it has been recited at numerous civil rights meetings and on many other occasions; and, in recent years, it has appeared in several anthologies.

Tolson was elated when "Dark Symphony" won the contest, and he sent Calverton a copy of the poem. Several mornings later he was crossing the Wiley campus when a student approached with a telegram. Tolson recalled that the dazzling brightness of the sun made his head spin as he read the message from Calverton's wife: V. F. Calverton was dead from leukemia at the age of forty. Tolson thought of their last parting when he had said, "Till we meet again," and Calverton had replied strangely, "Where?" Now Tolson wondered if his friend had known this farewell was their last one. "The Man Inside," which appears in Tolson's first book of poetry, commemorates his feelings about the friend who drew him "into the catholic Evermore." The poem, named for a book by Calverton, concludes: "We stood on common ground, in transfiguring light,/Where the man inside is neither Black nor White." [13]

Tolson's ability to judge men on an individual basis rather than on the basis of their color saved him from the bitterness and hatred felt by many victims of injustice. He was not, however, a man to "turn the other cheek"; and he was dedicated to the cause of the masses. Many mornings he arrived home just as his children were leaving for school, but only years later did they learn of the dangerous all-night meetings at which their father had helped organize poor sharecroppers, both black and white.[14] Tolson's experiences served as the background for his poem "Ballad of the Rattlesnake," which appears in *Rendezvous*. He admitted that he did not know how he had escaped being lynched. An ex-president of Wiley College once told him, "Many times I heard that you were speaking in those little towns and I thought I'd hear the next morning that a teacher was hanging on a tree." An article which appeared in the Chicago *Defender* after the publication of Tolson's first book comments that most Negro college students in the Deep South either knew Tolson personally or had heard of him and "of his fearlessness before lynch mobs." As an aside, the reviewer mentioned that "one Texan who led a mob against him later gave a piano to his Little Theatre." [15]

Without doubt, Tolson's speeches made some of his audiences uncomfortable, particularly those persons responsible for inviting him. He was a dynamic orator—many who have heard him speak find it difficult to say whether he was a better speaker or poet—and some of his debaters at Wiley told him, "Doc, if we had your gifts, we'd be the richest politicians around." Tolson lacked the diplomacy of many politicians, however. At a Gladewater High School commencement one spring, when the black principal asked Tolson to sit down because he was talking too long, Tolson took one look at the restless white superintendent and knew what had determined the request. At the end of another commencement address in a little Louisiana town which had been the site a short time before of a multiple lynching, only two or three uneasy people attended the reception given in honor of the guest speaker. Each time a car drove by, everyone rushed to the window. Finally, Tolson and the Wiley College student who had driven him down, Benjamin Bell, decided to leave by the back road, much to the relief of their hosts. The next morning they learned that the mob had been waiting for them on the main highway. On still another occasion, Tolson was ordered to the police station by an outraged deputy—not for an inflammatory speech but for passing a white driver with his car. While Tolson's small children sat trembling in the car, the deputy threatened to whip their father for his audacity. Tolson did not reply to the deputy, but addressed his remarks calmly to the sheriff, who eventually let him go with a warning.[16]

In spite of these harrowing experiences, Tolson kept his sense of humor, admitting that he had some stereotyped concepts himself. In one of his classroom lectures, he recalled that one evening at Wiley College when he was to share the platform with a quartet and a visiting black soloist named Chief Tecumseh, he had meandered over to the auditorium early to meet the visitors. Chief Tecumseh introduced his accompanist, the first Eskimo that Tolson had ever met. Immediately, he said, there came to his mind the story of the missionary who had given a bar of soap to an Eskimo—who thanked him for it and ate it.

V *Publication of* Rendezvous with America

Tolson's literary career was launched with the publication of his first book of poems in 1944, *Rendezvous with America*. The book was well received, and several thousand reprints of the title poem were made; one women's organization requested fifteen hundred copies. It appeared in magazines and newspapers, was used in a national bond drive on the Pacific coast, and was studied by interracial study groups throughout the country. Later, it was set to music. William Rose Benét called *Rendezvous* "remarkable" and "exciting" in an article in *Saturday Review* and said that Tolson had "the insurrection in him of the real poet." [17] Tolson was pleased with the reviews of *Rendezvous*, but he was still looking for the style which was right for him. He was slowly overcoming his prejudices against modern poetry and was fascinated with the possibilities it offered to one with his literary background and love of word study. A few years before, while browsing in a Harlem bookstore, he had overheard a white couple discussing a first edition of T. S. Eliot's *The Waste Land* and had read it out of curiosity. Immediately he was struck by the style, particularly the "inverted participial phrase, because I was grounded in grammar, and I knew Eliot was 'doing something.' " [18]

Tolson's lifelong fascination with grammar emerged also in a pamphlet entitled "Forty Uses of the Noun," which he composed for his students. His dictionary was his constant companion and the primary textbook for every class he taught. His mind was saturated with the classics of various literatures. It is not surprising, therefore, that Eliot's style—characterized by numerous allusions, symbols, images, and grammatical forcefulness—appealed to him and exerted influence on the style Tolson was developing. A letter of rejection he received from the poetry editor of *Mainstream* in 1946 indicates his stylistic tendencies at that time. The editor criticized Tolson for making confusing references, for cramming too much into the poem, for telescoping language, and for being obscure. Such criticism did little, however, to curb these tendencies; for he was on his way with the difficult, allusive style which flowered in *Libretto to the Republic of Liberia* (1953).

VI   *Langston University Years Produce* Libretto *and* Harlem Gallery

In 1947, Tolson decided to move from Wiley College, where he had begun his teaching career, to another small college for black students, Langston University, which is located approximately fifty miles north of Oklahoma City, Oklahoma. He taught at Langston until his retirement in 1964. The esteem with which Tol-

son was regarded by many persons at Wiley College may be noted
in an editorial which appeared in the Wiley *Reporter* shortly after
Tolson had moved to Langston, Oklahoma, to assume his duties
as professor of English and drama and as director of the Dust-
bowl Players at Langston University. The article stated in part:

> Tolson was more than an instructor at Wiley: he was a part of
> Wiley College. . . . There is no forgetting his "Voice in the
> Wilderness." Nor is there any forgetting his love for dramatics and
> his dream of a "Little Log Cabin Theatre" on Wiley's campus.
> . . . It would be a fitting tribute to finish this Little Log Cabin
> Theatre and dedicate it to him.
>   Monuments are only for the great, and after tracing thru [*sic*]
> the records of Wiley's history, we find few men of greater stature
> than the radical little man who brought undying fame to Wiley as
> a debate coach, lecturer, author, instructor, and personality.
> Thousands went thru [*sic*] Wiley during his time: they have not
> forgotten. Nor have the countless others who saw his plays and
> players, heard his debate teams, and read his works. Numerous
> cities will accept with open arms any group having sincere loyalty
> to him. This is a worthy cause. Let's build a monument to it.[19]

The monument was never built, but Tolson's move to Langston
University in 1947 initiated a new era in his writing career: in this
year he was named poet laureate of Liberia, and he began the
major task of composing a poem of tribute to Liberia. The stylistic
characteristics which had been manifested in *Rendezvous* had
matured in the decade which elapsed between the appearance of
his first and his second book of poetry; and *Libretto* (1953) reveals the depth and scope of his cultural, historical, religious,
philosophical, and literary resources. Lorenzo Turner in a review
in *Poetry* magazine states that the *Libretto* "is not merely an occasional poem. In its breadth, in the subtlety and richness of its
allusions, and in the force and suggestiveness of its language, it is
a triumph of poetry on the grand scale." [20] Shortly after the publication of *Libretto*, John Ciardi nominated Tolson for a Bread
Loaf Fellowship, calling him "the most rocket-driven poet we
have published" and commenting: "The one thing about Tolson is that he is incapable of writing a mediocre line: it's either
tremendous or it's nothing." [21] Tolson accepted the invitation to

Bread Loaf which he subsequently received; and here he met Robert Frost, who promised to visit the Tolsons at Langston on the occasion of Tolson's retirement. Frost did not live to keep this promise, but Tolson never forgot the warmth and wit of the great poet who spent several hours conversing with him.

Since Tolson had always found it necessary to teach full time to support his family, he had long since formed the habit of sleeping the first part of the night, waking around midnight, and working for several hours. This schedule provided the only time he could manage for writing since his work called for teaching, directing all dramatic productions, and attending teachers' meetings and committee meetings—when he had to do so. In addition, he was a popular speaker for all kinds of programs throughout the South and Southwest. Although it was difficult to find time to write, he had to try; for, as he observed, "The urge to write is as powerful as the drives of sex and hunger. Here is a good piece of dialogue you have done. You know the thrill of Columbus when he saw that light shining across the unknown ocean. The old typewriter rattles again. Perhaps. Perhaps. Perhaps!" [22]

During this busy time Tolson directed such plays as Frederick Knotts' *Dial 'M' for Murder*, Lorraine Hansberry's *A Raisin in the Sun*, Ruth and Augustus Goetz's *The Heiress*, an adaptation of James Hilton's novel *Lost Horizon*, and Jean Paul Sartre's *No Exit*, as well as his own highly publicized dramatization of Walter White's *The Fire in the Flint*. His interest in writing poetry did not wane in the midst of these time-consuming activities, and in 1952 he was named recipient of the Bess Hokim Award by *Poetry* magazine for his long psychological poem "E. & O.E." The following year *Libretto* was published; and on January 11, 1954, the Liberian government honored him by sponsoring a literary tea at the Liberian embassy in Washington, D.C. Four months later, Ambassador Simpson conferred upon him a distinction which admitted him to the Knighthood of the Order of the Star of Africa.[23] Later, Ambassador Simpson visited the poet laureate at Langston University; and in 1956 Tolson was invited to attend President Tubman's inauguration in Liberia at the expense of the Liberian government.

An unpretentious person, Tolson was impressed by the detailed instructions concerning proper dress and protocol for the inaugu-

ration. When he arrived, the various personalities of those he met
fascinated him; and he was entertained by their reactions to him.
The Soviet ambassador to Liberia seemed quite awed by the fact
that he was a poet; but the Liberian chiefs, who paid little attention to his poet laureate title, honored him as mayor of Langston.
Even this political office failed to impress one old chief when he
learned that Tolson had only one wife: the chief had eight wives,
and he inquired subtly whether America had any kula nuts, a del-
icacy similar to snuff which reputedly bolstered virility. Before
returning home, Tolson went to France on what proved to be his
only trip abroad. Here he visited his son Melvin, Jr., who was
working toward a diploma in contemporary literature at the Sor-
bonne.

The Tolsons were in Langston three years before moving into
the white frame house just off Highway 33, where they lived until
his retirement. In 1954, he was elected mayor of Langston; and he
served four consecutive terms, hoping he could do something to
improve conditions in the all-black community; but there was little money to work with. Moreover, every time someone wanted a
street light placed in front of his house, he consulted the mayor;
and Tolson's family finally encouraged him to give up a position
which not only was frustrating but was also absorbing too much
of the time he could devote to his writing.

Tolson's students, with whom he enjoyed conversing, took
much of his time, also; his courses were popular ones—indeed, it
was an unwritten law at Langston University that every student
should take at least one course with Professor Tolson. No matter
what the name of the course, it included far more than the title
implied. The notebook of a student in one of his English literature
classes[24] contains the following statements on diverse subjects, a
few of which fall within the realm of English literature:

The Round Table was a symbol of social equality.

Forms of definitions: authority, exemplification, explication, implication, analogy.

"If you don't know where you came from, you don't know where
you're going." (Lincoln)

"The lie of the artist is the only lie for which a mortal or a god
should die." (Picasso)

Every person is a tridimensionality: biological, sociological, psychological.

3 Ages of Man: Exploration, Exploitation, Explanation.

Tolson's method of teaching made an indelible impression on the many students who passed through his classroom. An actor who performed wherever there was an audience, he kept his students guessing as to what the hour would hold. He might jump up on his desk and lecture from there, order two students to dance to the meter of a poem, or spin a series of tales about famous persons he had known. Whatever the subject, it always ended up as philosophy; and he made sure that his students left his classes with a "black is beautiful" concept long before the phrase was put into those words and popularized. A fanatic about vocabulary-building, Tolson often declared that the only difference between a bank president and a janitor was the vocabulary of each. Some days he would call on a student who could not define one of the erudite terms that he delighted in using and teaching the class; and then the show began—to the delight of the class *and* the student who was about to be showered with attention for the next few minutes:

Jones, Jones! I'm so *glad* you came to this university! I'm so glad you're in *my* class! What if you'd gone to some other college and revealed all that compounded ignorance! Girls, take a good look at this poor boy from the backwoods. Don't you marry him or the one just like him sitting next to you. You wait till you get your degree! It's far better to spend your honeymoon in the Waldorf Astoria than in Joe's Motel, and don't you forget it. Now, Jones, explain to the class how it's possible for a student to live eighteen years, spend twelve of them in an educational institution, and arrive at college so completely uninformed about the English language.

This type of tirade would be accompanied by a ferocious scowl, arm-waving, desk-pounding—"the works." It was an honor to be singled out by Tolson as the horrible example of the day, however, for the student knew he was a favorite. No teacher cared more for his students than Tolson, and his papers contain many letters of appreciation and gratitude from his students which testify to his effectiveness as a teacher and as a friend.

Another method Tolson used to send the students in the direction of the library was to appeal to racial pride. He demanded excellence, was quick to praise when students worked, and ready to lambaste when they did not. One diatribe, according to a student who had two or three courses with him, went like this: "You know, I believe some of you students have heard that if you study hard you'll go crazy. Don't you know that's a hangover from slavery? Your grandpa had the choice of being a preacher, a teacher, an undertaker, or a bum. From the looks of these papers, I'd say that you're settling for the last choice, even though the professions are wide open to you today. You know where white folks put information they want to hide from you? Books and magazines and newspapers—that's where!" [25] The desired result was a general exodus to the library. One of his speech students has said of him, "I've decided to strive for excellence because Dr. Tolson made me see that mediocrity is not good enough." [26]

After over forty years of orating to and debating with his students, Tolson was quite at ease with the various audiences of eminence he faced during his last two years. He chuckled as he told his students at Langston when he was invited to speak in the Library of Congress, "You know how I like to talk. There's nothing I enjoy more. And those white folks are going to *pay* me to talk. Yes, I think I can talk *well* for $500 an hour." [27]

When Tolson had completed the *Libretto*, he felt as if he had put the best of himself into the long ode. In only a matter of months, however, he began to think of the old manuscript of Harlem portraits which he had scrapped several years before. At first, he toyed with the problem of how to weave the characters into a story; then he conceived the idea of a great epic work which would narrate the story of the black man in America from the early 1600's to the present. He envisioned a five-volume work: *Harlem Gallery: Book I, The Curator; Book II, Egypt Land; Book III, The Red Sea; Book IV, The Wilderness;* and *Book V, The Promised Land.* This undertaking was unique and ambitious, and Tolson was an artist who refused to be hurried. He spent the next eleven years writing and polishing *Harlem Gallery: Book I, The Curator* while he was completing his teaching career at Langston University. When he had revised the manuscript to his satisfaction, he felt that he had met the standard he had set for himself as an artist. He had envisioned the Harlem gallery of his people in the style in which he could work most artistically. Book I was the only volume to be completed before his death, however. Like several other lengthy works in American literature—Hart Crane's *The Bridge,* William Carlos Williams' *Paterson,* and perhaps Ezra Pound's *Cantos*—the influence the complete work would have had can be only a matter of conjecture.

The illness which cut short Tolson's work struck without warning. Tolson was a healthy, dynamic person with boundless energy; and in his later years when his children returned home for visits, he kept them up all night talking or until they pleaded exhaustion.[28] He observed the precaution of having periodic checkups since there was a history of cancer in his family; but, when he suffered severe abdominal pains in the spring of 1964, he little suspected anything other than the gallstones which his doctor insisted on removing. In April, he entered the hospital in nearby Guthrie, Oklahoma, for the operation. His family was hardly prepared for the news that he had an abdominal malignancy and had only about six months to live. Tolson read the truth in their faces, then announced that he had too much work to do to die, and asserted that he would show the doctor that he was wrong. One of his students suggested a cancer specialist in Dallas. Tolson went to see him; and the specialist, Dr. William Strickland, prolonged his life for two years.

Before the April operation, Tolson had been reading the proof of *Harlem Gallery;* and time dragged as he waited for it to be published. In September, he began his final year of teaching before retirement; but his health declined steadily. Shortly before the Christmas holidays, he made an appointment to enter St. Paul's Hospital in Dallas for a second operation, which followed the first one by only eight months. Although he feared he would not live to see *Harlem Gallery* in print, few persons fathomed his state of mind. At the English Club Christmas party just before the holidays, he joined his students on the dance floor, joking and entertaining as usual and reminiscing about his old friend W. C. Handy when the combo played "The St. Louis Blues."

The operation was performed a few days later, and he lay in a weakened condition in early January when Karl Shapiro's prepublication review of *Harlem Gallery* appeared in the New York *Herald Tribune.* No better medicine could have been prescribed, for Shapiro had heralded *Harlem Gallery* as a work "improvised by one of the great architects of modern poetry," predicting that "this work, like other works of its quality in the past, will turn out to be not only an end in itself but the door to poetry that everyone has been looking for." [29] Miraculously, Tolson was back in the classroom by February. President William H. Hale and Tolson's chairman, Mrs. Moxye W. King, arranged a first-floor classroom for him, but the irrepressible little professor could not stay there when most of his colleagues had offices on the second floor. It was a familiar sight to see him slipping upstairs in his red house shoes—the one concession he made to his convalescent state.

Tolson rather enjoyed his role as campus character. When someone commented about his unique methods of teaching or about his all-embracing course content, he replied that he was merely trying to teach his students "how to ape instead of monkey." At the final commencement exercise in which he participated at Langston University, he dashed up, late as usual, to join the moving line of faculty members in academic regalia as they marched into the auditorium, his tassel half on one side of his cap and half on the other. One of his colleagues shook his head and smiled, "Look at that Tolson. Sometimes I think that man must have gotten his degree from the University of Mars." And Tolson contributed to the myth by telling stories about himself. One of his favorites was a true story about a neighbor in Langston, who, when asked by one of his former students what "Prof" Tolson was doing these days, replied, "Oh, he's still typin'."

But to the surprise of Tolson's neighbors—and of Tolson—when *Harlem Gallery* went on sale in March, 1965, he was invited to New York, Philadelphia, and Washington, D.C., where he began to receive a long overdue tribute from the literary world. Langston University honored him by dedicating the spring Fine Arts Festival to him, and Karl Shapiro came to Langston to share the podium and pay tribute to him. Langston University audiences and guests from nearby towns and universities enjoyed two delightful evenings of poetry recited by the two poets.

At the university retirement banquet on May 17, Tolson again had a captive audience. The guests gasped with laughter as he described the shocked expression on a fellow teacher's face a few days previously when he had approached the poet in the hall, taken him aside, and whispered: "Tolson, have you been lecturing to your students with your pants unzipped!" He had looked him straight in the eye and replied, "Colleague, I teach my students to look up. And if you as a professor at Langston University would do the same, you would never have seen my unzipped pants!" Adroitly changing the mood, Tolson told the group that, had death not taken his friend Robert Frost, he would have shared this evening of his retirement with them as he had promised. Tolson then remarked, "Now I, like Frost, have 'miles to go before I sleep.' For my fellow teachers who are retiring and me, the important thing is not that we are old, but how we look, the stance we take." He concluded with a quotation from Tennyson's "Ulysses":

> I cannot rest from travel; I will drink
> Life to the lees . . . you and I are old;
> Old age hath yet his honor and his toil
> Death closes all; but something ere the end,
> Some work of noble note, may yet be done.

VII *Poet-in-Residence at Tuskegee Institute*

Like Ulysses, Tolson could not retire. When he received an invitation to become the first poet-in-residence at Tuskegee Institute, he could not refuse. In October, 1965, he also became one of the first black poets to speak under the auspices of the Gertrude Clarke Whittall Poetry and Literature Fund at the Library of Congress. The Liberian ambassador gave a reception in his honor at the Liberian embassy in November. Tolson had more speaking engagements than he could fill, and he was trying to complete his research on the history of the Afro-American so that he could get Book II of his five-volume epic underway. The morning after his appearance at the Library of Congress in October, however, he had to fly to Dallas where a third operation was performed. He returned to the classroom at Tuskegee despite the protests of his family and friends. He also accepted some speaking engagements; and, when he spoke, it was with the same vigor which had always marked his talks. Those who heard his address at the Oklahoma State University Arts and Sciences Banquet in Stillwater in February, 1966, scarcely thought that the dynamic philosopher-poet who talked about "The Ladder of the Mind" had only six months to live.

In April, Tolson was one of the speakers at the Fisk University Centennial Writers' Conference on "The Image of the Negro in

American Literature." David Llorens described the enthusiasm which Tolson generated there in an article published in *Negro Digest:* "One attends a writers' conference anticipating new ideas, pertinent criticisms, enhanced perspectives—a touch of the inexplicable as well as the profound—but one also secretly hopes for that person who will rise to the occasion and provide the emotional stimulus that transforms writers' conferences into good old "down home" Baptist conventions—for at least a little while! That stimulus was provided by Melvin B. Tolson, the man described by Karl Shapiro as 'The Poet Who Writes in Negro.' . . ." Llorens' article then describes how Tolson, following Robert Hayden, a well-known black poet who insists that he is "a poet who happens to be a Negro,"

> rose from his chair with the energy of one of his pupils, and in a sweeping gesture and a booming voice that rocked Jubilee Hall, he roared: "Nobody writes in a vacuum or out of a vacuum—when a man writes, he tells me which way he went in society."
>
> The audience, now spellbound, listened as the man who might affectionately be called the grandfather of the conference spoke of the tridimensionality of Man: "A man has his biology, his sociology, and his psychology—*and then he becomes a poet.*"
>
> Glancing over his shoulder at Hayden, the grin on his face reminiscent of a mischievous lad, once again Tolson's tone was soft, almost reverent, "'Hap, hap . . . let me see, hap means accident. Is someone going to make M. B. Tolson an accident? You'll never make me an accident," and by this time his voice was blazing to the rafters as he exclaimed:
>
> "I'm a black poet, an African-American poet, a Negro poet. I'm no accident—and I don't give a tinker's damn what you think." [30]

One of Tolson's finest moments occurred in New York City on the evening of May 25 when George Kennan, president of the American Academy of Arts and Letters, presented him with the annual poetry award. He recognized Tolson's tremendous breadth and scope with these words: "His poetry of Negro life and America, conceived on an epic scale, is at once bitter and laughing, colloquial and erudite, jazzy and philosophical."

But Tolson's time was running out. He and Ruth returned to their modest home in Langston to keep one more date before he returned to Dallas for the checkup he had postponed as long as possible. All the Tolsons attended commencement exercises at the University of Oklahoma in early June to see a family dream come true: Arthur became the third Tolson son to attain the doctoral degree. Although Tolson was proud of his sons, as well as of his wife and daughter, both of whom had master's degrees, he delighted in confiding to his audiences, "I keep telling my boys, 'It doesn't matter how many doctor's degrees you boys get—you won't ever catch up with your old man. He has a headstart on you—and as long as he's around he intends to keep it.' "

A few days after the commencement, Tolson entered St. Paul's Hospital for the last time. He remained there for two months, while Dr. Strickland performed three more operations in a desperate attempt to prolong his life. Tolson was stoic, even optimistic, through the torturous weeks; for, when his friends and relatives called or visited him, he talked not about his illness but about the work he planned to do. A colleague of his at Langston University who phoned him often recalled that he spoke only once of his impending death: he said wistfully that he wished someone—or perhaps the state of Oklahoma—would put a marker by his home in Langston, indicating that an Oklahoma poet had lived there.

On August 29, 1966, at the age of sixty-six, Melvin Beaunorus Tolson died in Dallas, Texas. In the I. W. Young auditorium at Langston University, where so many audiences had heard him speak during his eighteen-year tenure there, the college chaplain, Dr. John L. Coleman, and the poet's colleagues and friends paid tribute to him in a simple religious ceremony; and he was buried in the Summit View Cemetery on the outskirts of Guthrie, Oklahoma, on September 3, 1966.

In the Page Library Annex at Langston University there is now a Melvin B. Tolson Room, which is a repository for a collection of black literature and art; and the Langston University Creative Writers' Club is raising money to erect a marker near his home. So far, however, the only marker in the area which bears his name is the redstone tombstone on the northeast side of the cemetery in Guthrie. It looks eastward, where fifteen miles away lie his former home and the university in which he taught while he wrote two of the three books which have established a place for him among twentieth-century American poets.

VIII   *Questions About Tolson the Poet*

Tolson had intended to write his autobiography—and a fascinating story it was he had to tell. An unforgettable character himself, he had toured the country with W. C. Handy; addressed audiences with Langston Hughes everywhere from college auditoriums to county jails; drunk tea with W. H. Auden while conversing loudly over the rumble of a protesting stomach because he had little supposed that Auden's invitation to tea meant tea and no more; and weathered a hurricane in the company of Robert Frost.

But, when Tolson's family and friends tried to persuade him to jot down the important events of his life or to tape some of his experiences just in case the autobiography did not materialize—and it became increasingly apparent during the last two years of his life that it would not—he refused to cooperate. His son Arthur tried to tape some of the anecdotes which emerged in family conversations, but the click of the tape recorder signaled the end of these sessions. Melvin, Jr., said, "It was as if he felt that a biography or autobiography is the last thing one does—and he intended to postpone that final work as long as possible." Tolson protested to a would-be biographer that he did not have the materials organized, that he wanted everything in order before beginning the work.

Now this statement was a discouraging one because Tolson was a highly disorganized person. As he went about the campus, he left his briefcase in his classroom; a half-finished cigar (about which he would inquire later) in his chairman's office, where he had just spent forty-five minutes explaining why he had failed to fill out quadruplicate copies of a leave-of-absence form before going to Florida to judge a speech tournament six weeks previously; and his horn-rimmed spectacles ($1.00 dime-store variety), over which he peered as he read or straightened out an errant student, on a colleague's desk. The countless pages of metaphors and allusions he had collected for years were spread all over the Zulu Club, the basement room in his home where he wrote and entertained the numerous friends who frequently invaded. But no one could out-argue the master debater whose final rebuttal was always: "Now you know it's not the poet's life that's important. It's the work. It's my work you should be studying and writing about. You'll find the man in the work anyway. A man's a jack-in-the-box. His actions aren't consistent, and you can't explain what he's done or predict what he'll do. But analyze his writing carefully and you'll have him. There's where you'll find the distilled essence of the man."

And Tolson was right as far as his own work is concerned. In his poetry, the reader discovers Tolson's likes and dislikes, as well as his attitude toward people and life in general. The reader sees that, though Tolson's style of writing changed dramatically through the years, his basic values remained the same. To be sure, if one approaches the work with a knowledge of the psychological and sociological pressures which helped shape these values, he finds himself better equipped to answer those questions which occur to him: Why did Tolson produce only three books of poetry during his sixty-six years? What delayed for so many years the development of a style which was satisfactory to him? How does his pattern of development differ from that of other contemporary literary figures? Why is it difficult to compare his work with that of other poets of significance, both black and white? How is he regarded today by both black and white critics? What is his place in contemporary literature? To find the answers to these and other questions which may arise, one must examine the work carefully; for there he finds, as Tolson said, "the distilled essence of the man."

CHAPTER *2*

Rendezvous with America

A squash grows up
At a summer's stroke;
An age wears out
To make an oak.
—Tolson, "A Scholar Looks at an Oak"

WHEN Tolson's "Dark Symphony" won first place in the National Poetry Contest sponsored by the American Negro Exposition in 1940, it gave him his first opportunity to make a mark in the literary world. The poem appeared in the September, 1941, issue of *Atlantic Monthly* and attracted the attention of various critics, including Mary Lou Chamberlain, assistant editor of the periodical. Later, when she joined Dodd, Mead and Company as an editor, she asked Tolson to collect some of his poems for a book. He had on hand "Dark Symphony"; a long poem entitled "Rendezvous with America," which had been published in the 1942 summer issue of *Common Ground;* two or three sonnets; and a few other poems. He was teaching full time, but he completed enough poems for a book during the summer months. The letter of acceptance of his manuscript arrived on Christmas Eve of 1943.

Rendezvous with America, which was named for one of the major poems in the volume, was published in 1944. Several excellent poems appear in the collection, some of which were written much earlier; therefore, the book offers insight into Tolson's development as a poet. As has been observed, Tolson had initiated his career as a poet some thirty years prior to this time by imitating great poets. A Shakespearian sonnet, a Whitmanesque compilation of descriptive detail in free verse, a series of words with onomatopoetic effects like Poe's,[1] lines vibrating with the rhythms of Vachel Lindsay—these seemed to him to be worthy exercises for an aspiring young poet.

Since childhood, Tolson had read and absorbed great literature; and his ambition, far-fetched though it might have seemed at the time, had been to make the poetry of Melvin B. Tolson, black poet, worthy of inclusion in anthologies with the work of the poets whom he emulated. For as long as he could remember, he had also wanted to help the cause of the downtrodden peoples of the world, especially his own people. Enthralled by the Muse and proud of his heritage as an Afro-American poet, his dream was to acquaint his readers with the accomplishments of the black man, as well as with his history of endurance and long-suffering, so that everyone might understand and appreciate the significant contributions the black man had made, and is continuing to make, to America and to the world.

Versifying came easily to Tolson. He could have joined the line of folk bards whose poems he enjoyed, but for him to attain the artistic standard he set for himself early in life required several decades of intensive study and work. Whenever he was discouraged, he would tell himself: "In the kingdom of poetry, there are many mansions. The Negro, in his illiteracy, has produced some of our greatest lyrics as he told of tragedy in his history. But there are fewer real poets in the Negro race than in any other, and for this reason, the most precious thing in the Negro race is a poet." [2]

When *Rendezvous* appeared, several critics called attention to his mastery of traditional form. Margaret Walker wrote that he "handles difficult metres with comparative ease." [3] Nathaniel Tillman was equally complimentary: "Professor Tolson seems to show a finer mastery of traditional poetic form than most of the recent Negro poets. He handles the quatrain, long or short line, with virtuosity. And he exhibits excellent technique in the twelve Shakespearian sonnets which comprise a section of the volume. Particularly effective are his cryptic final couplets." [4]

I *Manipulation of Traditional Form*

As Tillman's statements make clear, *Rendezvous* contains a number of different types of poems with diversity of form.

The poems in *Rendezvous* also reflect Tolson's interest both in art and in music. Just a few months before his death he confessed to an audience, "I'm frustrated twice. I'm a frustrated musician and a frustrated artist. But I went back to music and art in my poems." [5] As a result of his interest in music and art, Tolson incorporated both art forms in the formula for writing poetry which he developed in the 1930's and which he called his "three S's of Parnassus"—*sight, sound,* and *sense. Sight* referred to the appearance of the poem on the page; *sound,* to the sound of the words (an element which he tested as he wrote by pacing the floor and reciting the lines loudly, regardless of the hour); *sense,* to the image, the appeal to the senses. He also relied on his knowledge of grammar and sentence construction in determining the varied line length as his poetry began to move away from conventional form.

Although the poems in *Rendezvous* are rooted in traditional style, Tolson often departs from restrictions which such form imposes; and, with the tools of sight, sound, and sense, he effects originality of style. He leans heavily on his "three S's of Parnassus" to bring forth originality out of metrical diversity.

Because the poems in *Rendezvous* vary both in subject matter and form, they are difficult to categorize. The 121-page book is divided into eight sections. Each of the four longer poems—"Rendezvous with America," "Dark Symphony," "The Idols of the Tribe," and "Tapestries of Time"—forms a unit. Most of the shorter poems are categorized by content, though one section consists of twelve sonnets which range in subject from the poet's grade-school teacher, who, with "the miracle of his integrity/Put bone and blood and soul into girl and boy" ("The Gallows," 60), to a Malayan guide on a jungle path, who comments, as he watches a python's coils pile up "high and dense" around the white man whose curse had obscured his warning: "Sahib, the blindness of scorn provokes offense" ("The Blindness of Scorn," 61). Other poems appear in sections entitled "Woodcuts for Americana," "A Song for Myself," and "Of Men and Cities."

Some of the poems in *Rendezvous* seem to have been exercises in poetic technique which Tolson regarded as a challenge, and one of these is "A Song for Myself." Tolson was quite proud that Robert Hillyer had called it a "tour de force" in a New York *Times* review which heralded him as "a good poet and a good craftsman as well." [6] It consists of twenty-two eight-line stanzas in which the poet sets forth some fundamental truths as he sees them concerning mankind in general and himself in particular. The opening lines illustrate how content and form blend to capture the reader's

interest. The unique form draws attention to the uniqueness of the
author of these lines:

> I judge
> My soul
> Eagle
> Nor mole:
> A man
> Is what
> He saves
> From rot.
>
> The corn
> Will fat
> A hog
> Or rat:
> Are these
> Dry bones
> A hut's
> Or throne's?
> (45)

These two sentences exhibit characteristics found throughout Tolson's work: juxtaposition of biblical and literary phrases with
commonplace items or ideas to produce effective images and
metaphors, and the use of the commonplace to suggest the universal.

Much of Tolson's poetry presents in unique forms the injustices
suffered by the lower social classes, particularly the black man.
Some of the poems in *Rendezvous* tend toward rhetoric, but
in most of them his artistic control and technique prevent them
from being propagandistic. The subject of race works its way into
"A Song for Myself" in this stanza:

> If hue
> Of skin
> Trademark
> A sin,
> Blame not
> The *make*

For God's
Mistake.
(47)

Another poem which illustrates his ability to handle unusual stanzaic form is "The Furlough," an adaptation of the French *ballade*. The subject is unfaithfulness. A soldier on furlough, supposedly "an escalator to delight," resolves his jealous rage by choking his sweetheart to death: "Her beauty gathers rot on the golden bed,/The worst can happen only in the brain" (24). The stanzaic form can be observed in the opening quatrains:

> The worst can happen only in the brain:
>   I gaze upon her silken loveliness,
> She is a passion-flower of joy and pain
>   On the golden bed I came back to possess.
>
> I gaze upon her silken loveliness,
>   I image the intimacies of eager lovers
> On the golden bed I came back to possess.
>   The eye of jealousy midnight uncovers.
>   (23)

Even a preliminary reading of this poem leaves one with a number of memorable images, though such phrases as "silken loveliness" and "golden bed" may be regarded as conventional ones. The oral reader, however, is struck by the musical quality and rhythm of the words and phrases, though the content, which seems suited to a ballad or other traditional form more than to such a stylized form, reveals the poem to be primarily an exercise in prosody.

One of the best-known poems in the book is "Rendezvous with America," the title poem. The name of the poem indicates the poet's acknowledgment of his bond with his country, a tie which he makes explicit in the poem. The setting is the years of World War II, but the poem spans American history from the landing of the pilgrims at Plymouth Rock to the bombing of Pearl Harbor. In ten sections, the verse forms move the poem from one event to another; they change tone and pace as the poet characterizes his America, and the "3 S's"—sight, sound, and sense—combine with traditional form throughout the poem. Section I consists of eight-

een lines of free verse divided into seven- and eleven-line parts by
an italicized quatrain which exhibits meter and rhyme. The poem
begins,

> Time unhinged the gates
> Of Plymouth Rock and Jamestown and Ellis Island,
> And worlds of men with hungers of body and soul
> Hazarded the wilderness of waters,
> Cadenced their destinies
> With the potters'-wheeling miracles
> Of mountain and valley, prairie and river.
> > *These were the men*
> > *Who bridged the ocean*
> > *With arches of dreams*
> > *And piers of devotion:*
> Messiahs from the Sodoms and Gomorrahs of the Old World,
> Searchers for Cathay and Cipango and El Dorado . . . .
>
> > (3)

This excerpt reveals the poet's interest not only in the appearance of the lines on the page but also in imagery: "Time unhinged
the gates of Plymouth Rock . . ."; the immigrants spanned the
ocean with "arches of dreams" and "piers of devotion." He juxtaposes the biblical and historical past with the recent past—the
immigrants are "Messiahs from Sodom and Gomorrah," and so
forth. The sound is significant in unifying the lines and in empha-
sizing their rhythmical effect. "Sodom" and "Searchers" are alliterative, and "Cathay and Cipango" are alliterative visually. Both the
eye and ear respond to the eleven parallel phrases in the last part
describing the Pilgrim Fathers. The transition from free verse to
meter and then back to free verse also enhances the effectiveness
of the sound as well as the sight.

Part II is composed of five four-line stanzas of iambic tetrameter with the *aabb* rhyme scheme. The sound is emphasized by
rhythm, rhyme, and the repetition of the opening phrase in the
first line of each stanza, resulting in unity: "These were the
men. . . ." The first stanza reads,

> These were the men of many breeds
> Who mixed their bloods and sowed their seeds.

Designed in gold and shaped of dross,
They raised the Sword beside the Cross.

(3–4)

The several poetic devices at work here, along with the decided
metrical pattern, evoke emotion. In these four lines are found alliterative *m*'s, *b*'s, *s*'s, and *d*'s. Assonance appears in the various *o*
sounds: "dr*o*ss" and "Cr*o*ss"; "g*o*ld" and "Sw*o*rd." The lines are
rich in images and symbols, such as the "Sword" and "Cross." The
stress pattern, which exhibits little variation except for the opening trochaic foot in a predominantly iambic stanza, contrasts in-
terestingly with the free-verse section which follows.

Part III appeals to the sight. The first two free-verse sections
describe the immigration of various people to America. The first
line is longer than the following ones, which are indented:

Into the arteries of the Republic poured
        The babels of bloods,
        The omegas of peoples,
        The moods of continents,
        The melting-pots of seas,
        The flotsams of isms,
        The flavors of tongues,
        The yesterdays of martyrs,
        The tomorrows of utopias.

(4–5)

Here is a balance not only in the appearance of the lines but also
in the parallel construction of the eight subjects and of the prepositional phrases which follow them. Content and form blend as
the shorter lines suspend from the longer initial line. The poet's
lifelong fascination with words reveals itself in the numerous synonyms he lists throughout his poetry. Alliteration appears in several phrases, and assonance is apparent in the numerous *a*, *o*, and
e sounds. The third S of Tolson's trilogy, sense, is equally important; for the section contains many images.

In the concluding part, the poet rejoices in being an American;
and the rhythmical lines contain definitive metaphors rich with
imagery which suggests the harmonious interrelationship of the
peoples who call themselves Americans:

> America?
> America is the Black Man's country,
> The Red Man's, the Yellow Man's,
> The Brown Man's, the White Man's.
>
> America?
> An international river with a legion of tributaries!
> A magnificent cosmorama with myriad patterns and colors!
> A giant forest with loin-roots in a hundred lands!
> A cosmopolitan orchestra with a thousand instruments playing
> *America!*
>
> (5)

After reading this poem, a Southern newspaperman wrote, "Only a Negro whose spirit rises above so-called racial problems of to-day could write a poem so unprejudiced and so full of thankfulness to be an American, regardless of color, creed, or kind." [7]

Part IV changes from free verse to a predominantly iambic pentameter meter with an *abcb* rhyme scheme. The language is figurative as the poet characterizes ten famous Americans in the five quatrains. In this poem, which sings of the unity of Americans, the poet celebrates America's folk heroes—black and white, traditional and contemporary. The section begins,

> I see America in Daniel Boone,
> As he scouts in the Judas night of a forest aisle;
> In big Paul Bunyan, as he guillotines
> The timber avalanche that writhes a mile.
>
> (5)

Perhaps sense is the most noticeable of the three S's here; for, as the characters come alive, their heroic qualities raise them to the superman level. Treacherous dangers of blazing a trail in the wilderness face Daniel Boone in the "Judas night of a forest aisle," an image undergirded by the biblical allusion. Such connotative words as "guillotine," "avalanche," and "writhes" evoke visions of the forests hewn down by Paul Bunyan's ax. Other memorable images in Part IV picture Johnny Appleseed, whose "miracles/ Fruit the hills and valleys and plains of our Promised Land"; Joe DiMaggio, whose bat "cuts a vacuum in the paralyzed air";

and "brown Joe Louis, surfed in white acclaim." The use of the ballad stanza—varied though it is in lines two and four—connotes the feeling associated with the ballad hero.

Part V has five sections, and each defends people who have suffered scorn in America: the "kikes," the "dagos," the "chinks," the "bohunks," the "niggers." Unity results from the parallel structure of the free-verse quatrains, each of which is preceded by short three-line introductions. One section reads,

> A blind man said,
> "Look at the bohunks."
> And I saw
> Sikorsky blue-printing the cabala of the airways,
> Stokowski imprisoning the magic of symphonies with a baton,
> Zvak erecting St. Patrick's Cathedral in a forest of skyscrapers,
> Dvořák enwombing the multiple soul of the New World.
>
> (7)

This passage has an abundance of allusions; others range from "Brandeis opening the eyes of the blind to the constitution" to "Toscanini enchanting earthward the music of the spheres" (6, 7), perhaps a forced figure. And one also notes in these lines intensity in condensation: only a "blind man" would see "bohunks" rather than fellow men—not to mention the great individuals who have made important contributions to all mankind. Tolson manipulates words as he creates such parallel verbals as "enwombing" or changes a word's ordinary grammatical function. In so doing, he produces unique expressions; but he risks the danger of using phrases which appear to be contrived rather than inevitable. As William Rose Benét noted, "Sometimes Mr. Tolson uses words more for the love of their sound than for their aptitude. But he surprises with insight." [8] Tolson was steeped in traditional, prescriptive grammar, which may have caused him to use English as if it were an inflected language and which may have led him to the kind of syntax to which he sometimes resorts, such as consciously changing the function of a word.

Part VI changes once more from free verse to iambic pentameter with *aaba* rhyme scheme. In the five four-line stanzas, the first two lines of each picture the many faces of America, pointing out her weaknesses and strengths. Stanza three reads,

America can worship gods of brass
And bow before the strut of Breed and Class;
Then gather to her bosom refugees
Who champion the causes of the Mass.

(8)

Here the poet speaks through symbols such as "gods of brass," which carries the biblical connotation of the worship of idols and materialism. He personifies "breed" and "class," entities which he deplored; and he shows how Americans can be asinine one moment and then warmhearted and generous the next. Using the alliterative *b* sound in "*b*rass," "*b*ow *b*efore," "*B*reed," and "*b*osom," and *c* sound in "*C*lass," "*c*hampion," and "*c*auses," he also emphasizes the harshness of the initial *br* sound in "*br*ass and "*Br*eed." The opening lines of the quatrain have the chanting rhythm, though perhaps not the forcefulness, of some of Vachel Lindsay's strongly rhythmical lines which are heavily alliterative, as in "The Congo."

In Part VII, the three S's are again active. In twenty lines of five-stress and four-stress lines that abound with imagery, the poet pictures what happens when America sleeps:

Sometimes
Uncle Sam
Pillows his head on the Statue of Liberty,
Tranquilizes himself on the soft couch of the Corn Belt,
Laves his feet in the Golden Gate,
And sinks into the nepenthe of slumber.

And the termites of anti-Semitism busy themselves
And the Ku Klux Klan marches with rope and faggot
And the money-changers plunder the Temple of Democracy
And the copperheads start boring from within. . . .

(9)

In this passage Tolson breathes life into the "Uncle Sam" cliché as he develops the personification. The sleeping giant, content with his accomplishments, stretches over the land: the inert figure contrasts sharply with the active agents of vice. Figurative language and imagery appear in the passage.

This section should be read aloud for fullest effect—as should

all Tolson's poetry, for that matter. The verbs "pillows," "tranquilizes," and "laves" are connotative in their suggestion of the luxury
of idleness, an effect also achieved by the noun *nepenthe*. Alliteration appears in the *s* sounds. The whole stanza revolves
around the figure of Uncle Sam, the personification of America.

Part VIII is composed of three fifteen-line and one twenty-two
line metrical sections, and parallel structure marks each of the
three. Each begins with the line "I have a rendezvous with
America," and each contains eight or nine end rhymes at various
points. The three sections are broken by the one-word italicized
lines "*Here,/Now.*" The form of the last part is unusual:

> I have a rendezvous with America
> This Seventh of December.
> The maiden freshness of Pearl Harbor's dawn,
> The peace of seas that thieve the breath,
> I shall remember.
>   Then
> Out of yonder Sunrise Land of Death
> The fascist spawn
> Strikes like the talons of the mad harpoon,
> Strikes like the moccasin in the black lagoon,
> Strikes like the fury of the raw typhoon.
>   The traitor's ruse
>   And the traitor's lie,
>   Pearl Harbor's ruins
>   Of sea and sky,
>   Shall live with me
>   Till the day I die.
>   *Here,*
>   *Now,*
> At Pearl Harbor, I remember
> I have a rendezvous at Plymouth Rock and Valley Forge
> This Seventh of December.
>   (10–11)

Not only is there parallel structure among the parts, but the same
balance exists within the stanza. Lines three and four have similar
construction, as do lines nine, ten, and eleven. The six lines of
iambic dimeter (ll. 12–17) and the sharp accents of "*Here,/Now,*"
in lines eighteen and nineteen also reveal the poet's sense of form
and balance. Interrupting longer lines, the monosyllabic one-

word lines have almost the same metrical value as the lines preceding and following them. The combination of unpatterned metrical lines with those of patterned meter illustrates again how the poet has mastered and molded traditional form rather than limiting himself to its demands. Here also the S-trinity is at work.

Sound is important in this passage. Though the meter and length of line vary greatly, the lines have an irregular rhyme pattern: *xabcaxcbdddxexexexxaxa*. Equally significant is the rhythm, for the sudden transition from the unpatterned line of four or five stresses to the one-word line "Then" brakes the rhythm. The pace picks up in the following trochaic line (Coleridge's "tripping" meter), slows in the next (iambic dimeter), and gathers momentum with the three successive lines, which exhibit both end rhyme and parallel structure. Here the poet uses a variety of feet and additional unstressed syllables to move the line rapidly, achieving emphasis with the triplet:

Strikes like the	tálons	of the mád	harpoón,
Stríkes like the	mócassin	in the bláck	lagoón,
Stríkes like the	fúry	of the ráw	typhóon.

The repetition of the first word, *strike,* an action verb, and the initial dactyl shock the reader with forcefulness. Short lines of iambs and anapests follow the triplet. Then comes the accented pause—"*Here,/Now*"—and a resumption of the metrical form which initiated the stanza.

The *s* and *r* sounds appear repeatedly. The hissing *s* sound reinforces the serpent image summoned up by "spawn . . . Strikes . . . Strikes . . . Strikes" and is echoed later in "sea," "sky," and "shall." The *r* sound is similarly alliterated, and assonance and onomatopoeia charge the passage with emotion. Personification is another poetic device used in these lines: the poet has a "rendezvous with America"; Pearl Harbor's dawn has a "maiden freshness," with its connotation of Aurora; the mad harpoon has "talons"; the typhoon seethes with "fury." The three successive similes, in which anaphora is used with the repetition of "Strikes like," intensify the impact of the lines. The imagery appeals to almost all of the senses.

Parts IX and X are free verse. Part IX is composed of twenty lines; Part X, of sixteen. The sections personify the anatomical makeup of America. The first two examples of personification here are not so succcessful as the last two, in which the analogy is much clearer:

> . . . the brows of mountains
> And the breasts of rivers
> And the flanks of prairies
> And the wombs of valleys. . . .
>					(11)

Tolson lists in Whitmanesque style his nation's melodies, using musical terminology to enhance the imagery and an alternating *in-* and *and* pattern to set up the parallelism of the prepositional phrases:

> In the masculine allegro of factories
> And the blues rhapsody of express trains,
> In the bass crescendo of power dams
> And the nocturne adagio of river boats,
> In the sound and fury of threshing machines
> And the clarineting needles of textile mills,
> In the fortissimo hammers of shipyards
> And the diatonic picks of coal mines,
> In the oboe rhythms of cotton gins
> And the sharped notes of salmon traps,
> In the belting harmonics of lumber camps
> And the drumming derricks of oil fields. . . .
>					(11–12)

The poet's interest in music is obvious in the content of this stanza, as in much of his poetry, and also in the deft manipulation of rhythm. In the following passage, which concludes the poem, he combines personification and the simile to describe the physical attributes of America:

> America stands
> Granite-footed as the Rocky Mountains
> Beaten by the whirlpool belts of wet winds,
> Deep-chested as the Appalachians
> Sunning valleys in the palms of their hands,
> Tough-tendoned as the Cumberlands
> Shouldering the truck caravans of US 40,
> Clean-flanked as the lavender walls of Palo Duro

> Washed by the living airs of canyon rivers,
> Eagle-hearted as the Pacific redwoods
> Uprearing their heads in the dawns and dusks of ages.
> (12)

Again, his interest in parallelism of construction and in the use of synonyms is apparent. An early example of this trait appears in the forceful verbs and verbals in this stanza.

II *"Dark Symphony"*

"Dark Symphony," Tolson's most popular poem in *Rendezvous,* reflects his interest in music. The poem was eventually set to music by Earl Robinson, composer of "Ballad for Americans," a work which was sung and recorded by Paul Robeson. A literary reviewer for the Los Angeles *Times* said of "Dark Symphony" that "it not only voices the ideal of our times; it is also alive with what makes poetry for most of us—and that is music." [9]

Part I, *Allegro Moderato,* which consists of three quatrains of iambic pentameter with an *abab* rhyme pattern, sets the tone for the poem. The protagonist is the black American who owns his heritage proudly and who proclaims that he is the victim, not the villain, in American history. The poem opens by calling attention to a black American hero:

> Black Crispus Attucks taught
> > Us how to die
> Before white Patrick Henry's bugle breath
> Uttered the vertical
> > Transmitting cry:
> "Yea, give me liberty or give me death."
> (37)

The line placement attracts the eye, as the last words of lines one and three drop to form half lines for emphasis. The contrast of "Black Crispus Attucks" and "white Patrick Henry" also establishes the theme of the poem: the black man's contribution to his country, despite years of abuse from the white man, and the black man's gradual evolution to his place in the sun. The juxtaposition of history and literature—"No Banquo's ghost can rise/Against us now" (37)—continues to characterize Tolson's poetry, as does

vivid imagery: "Men black and strong . . . / Loin-girt with faith
that worms equate the wrong/And dust is purged to create broth-
erhood."

Part II, *Lento Grave*, slows to a rhythmical, unrhymed fourteen-
line section containing many unstressed syllables and long, melo-
dious vowel sounds, as the picture of the white man's inhumanity
is drawn clearly:

> The centuries-old pathos in our voices
> Saddens the great white world,
> And the wizardry of our dusky rhythms
> Conjures up shadow-shapes of ante-bellum years:
>
> Black slaves singing *One More River to Cross*
> In the torture tombs of slave-ships,
> Black slaves singing *Steal Away to Jesus*
> In jungle-swamps. . . .
>   (37–38)

Emotion is evoked in this passage laden with stylistic devices,
which include the alliterative *s, w,* and *t* sounds; onomatopoeia;
and the allusion to spirituals with their biblical connotations of
the children of Israel under their Egyptian captors, just as the
white slaveowners are referred to as "Southern Pharaohs" (38).

Part III, *Andante Sostenuto*, forms the transition from the black
slaves who sing "*Swing Low, Sweet Chariot*/ In cabins of death"
to their dark-skinned descendants who cannot forget—and this
section Tolson had written when he was in high school. Composed of three iambic-trimeter, eight-line stanzas with an
abcbdefe rhyme pattern, the section builds with the repetition of
"They tell us to forget" throughout the first two stanzas, employ-
ing emphatic variation to effect the climax with the repetition of
the question in stanza three: "Oh, how can we forget?"

> They tell us to forget
> The Golgotha we tread . . .
> We who are scourged with hate,
> A price upon our head.
> They who have shackled us
> Require of us a song,

> They who have wasted us
> Bid us condone the wrong.
>
> They tell us to forget
> Democracy is spurned.
> They tell us to forget
> The Bill of Rights is burned.
> Three hundred years we slaved,
> We slave and suffer yet:
> Though flesh and bone rebel,
> They tell us to forget!
>
> Oh, how can we forget
> Our human rights denied?
> Oh, how can we forget
> Our manhood crucified?
> When Justice is profaned
> And plea with curse is met,
> When Freedom's gates are barred,
> Oh, how can we forget?
>   (38–39)

As the section title indicates, the tempo accelerates in Part IV, *Tempo Primo*, which describes what was in 1944 more an ideal than a reality—the New Negro, who "strides upon the continent/In seven league boots . . ." (39). He is the son of Nat Turner, Joseph Cinquez, Frederick Douglass, Sojourner Truth, and Harriet Tubman. He is proud of his ancestors who lived to build this country and died to save it. Appropriately, free verse is employed in the four-part section, the last two parts of which characterize the "New Negro":

> His giant hands fling murals upon high chambers,
> His drama teaches a world to laugh and weep,
> His music leads continents captive,
> His voice thunders the Brotherhood of Labor,
> His science creates seven wonders,
> His Republic of Letters challenges the Negro-baiters.
>
> The New Negro,
> Hard-muscled, Fascist-hating, Democracy-ensouled,
> Strides in seven-league boots

Along the Highway of Today
Toward the Promised Land of Tomorrow!

(40)

Parallelism dominates the various stylistic devices used here. The long list of synonyms, similar to the one in the concluding section of "Rendezvous with America," appears in the third section: his ancestors "planted" crops, "built" ships, "erected" the Cotton Empire, "flung" railroads, "disemboweled" iron and coal, "tunneled" mountains, "bridged" rivers, "harvested" grain, "hewed" forests, "sentineled" the Thirteen Colonies, "unfurled" the flag, and "fought" for the Republic. Three parallel, hyphenated epithets describe the New Negro: "Hard-muscled, Fascist-hating, Democracy-ensouled." Again the part builds to a climax, this time by means of hyperbole, symbol, and allusion, as the New Negro "Strides in seven-league boots/Along the Highway of Today/Toward the Promised Land of Tomorrow!" Here, as in a few other instances in *Rendezvous,* Tolson turns in emotion-charged lines to conventional phrases which tend toward rhetoric designed primarily to stir the reader's feelings.

Part V, *Larghetto,* takes a backhanded slap at the failures of white Americans. Each of the four, six-line stanzas of rhymed *aabbcc* iambic trimeter and pentameter begins with the lines "None in the land can say/To us black men Today . . ." (40–41). The poet then lists events and conditions which Americans would like to forget: the "tractors on their bloody path" in Oklahoma (an allusion to John Steinbeck's *Grapes of Wrath*), slums, workers' empty dinner pails, stuffed ballot boxes, smashed stock markets, counterfeit Christianity, and fifth column plots. None of these, says the poet, is the work of the black man.

In the short concluding section, *Tempo di Marcia,* the New Negro emerges from the darkness of the past to take his place by the side of his fellow man. This section was perhaps more prophetic than realistic at the time it was written, but Tolson firmly believed in the progress of the black man and of his eventual recognition by all as an American citizen of the first rank:

Out of the abysses of Illiteracy,
Through labyrinths of Lies,

> Across waste lands of Disease. . .
> We advance!
>
> Out of dead-ends of Poverty,
> Through wildernesses of Superstition,
> Across barricades of Jim Crowism . . .
> We advance!
>
> (41–42)

One of the principal causes which Tolson espoused throughout his life was that of the common man. In the 1930's, he wrote, "I'm interested in the masses of men and women. And I feel better. I feel free. I sleep at night. I love everybody, in spite of the fact that you see me kicking the ask-me-no-questions of snobs and hypocrites and exploiters. I'm not fighting them personally. I'm fighting the ideas they represent—the dollar civilization they represent." [10] After a 1945 interview with Tolson, a reporter wrote, "He believes that Negroes must throw in their lot with the struggling masses and not isolate themselves on little islands of nationalism." [11] And only a year before his death, Tolson stated, "My approach is social . . . I am just as concerned by poverty among whites as among black folk. Blacks will never have genuine civil rights in the South, for example, until the white lower classes have been raised up and educated." [12] It is no accident, therefore, that the climactic lines of "Dark Symphony," a poem which "commemorates eighty years of Negro freedom," [13] state, "with the Peoples of the World . . . /We advance!"

Of the poems "Rendezvous with America" and "Dark Symphony," Nathaniel Tillman wrote that "Professor Tolson in his two sustained efforts, 'Rendezvous with America,' and 'Dark Symphony,' catches the full and free rhythmic swing and the shifting tempo of the verses of Walt Whitman—or of the late Stephen Vincent Benét. Both poems exhibit genuine poetic feeling, facility of expression, and vividness. The title poem, which is especially strong in imagery, is so apt an interpretation of and challenge to America that it deserves a lasting place in the anthologies of American literature." [14] These two poems, the best-known ones in Tolson's first book, employ the ode form on which he expanded in his two later books. Both *Libretto* and *Harlem Gallery* are long odes, but they are not conventional ones in form or in technique.

III   *"The Ballad of the Rattlesnake"*

A poem which Tolson almost always included whenever he presented a program of his poetry is "The Ballad of the Rattlesnake," the only ballad in *Rendezvous*. He sometimes introduced the poem by informing the audience with pride that poet-critic Paul Engle had considered it the best poem in the book. In the ballad, Tolson makes use of a legend about the Apaches, who on occasion tortured their white prisoners by staking them on the desert directly in front of a rattlesnake with a rock tied on its tail. The characters rise to the level of symbols in the ballad, a story within a story, which is narrated as a group of sharecroppers, both black and white, talk of what they have seen and heard. The story, like Emily Brontë's *Wuthering Heights,* is so intense that it requires a narrator to establish esthetic distance and to convey a sense of reality. The point of view is established in the two opening stanzas, which are repeated as the two concluding stanzas:

> *The sharecroppers sat*
> *In the Delta night;*
> *Many were black,*
> *And many were white.*
>
> *And this is the tale*
> *From the bearded mouth*
> *Of the dreamer who saw*
> *Green lands in the South.*
>
> The Apaches stake
> On the desert sands
> The blond man's feet
> And the blond man's hands.
>
> He curses and prays
> And tugs apace.
> The Apaches laugh
> And spit in his face.
>
> The blond man looks
> With gibbering breath

At the diamond coils
And the fangs of death.

The chief ties a rock
To the rattler's tail.
The blond man's blood
Congeals like hail.

The diamond head
Hisses and pries.
The horny tail
The rock defies.

As custom wills,
Bent like a bow,
The red chief stoops
And taunts his foe.

A madness crawls
In the rattler's brain:
The naked white thing
Is the cause of its pain.

At every lurch
The blond man dies.
Eternity ticks
Behind the eyes.

In the desert world
A scream tears space,
As the rattler strikes
The blond man's face.

Five miles away
The Apaches laugh
Like a frozen wind
In a crib of chaff.

The blond man lies
Like a bar of lead.
No hiss or laugh
Can vex the dead.

The desert holds
In its frying-pan
The bones of a snake
And the bones of a man.

And many a thing
With a rock on its tail
Kills the nearest thing
And dies by the trail.

The sharecroppers sat
In the Delta night;
Many were black,
And many were white.

And this is the tale
From the bearded mouth
Of the dreamer who saw
Green lands in the South.
                    (53–55)

The theme, made explicit in stanza fifteen, was quite appropriate to the 1960's and 1970's when riots in Watts, Detroit, Newark,
Chicago, and other cities have brought bloodshed and destruction
both to revolutionaries and to those around them. The poet was
militant in the sense that he worked and spoke for the rights of
oppressed peoples at a time when his actions could have resulted
in his being beaten or lynched. But he recognized hatred and bitterness as diseases which not only maim and kill but are self-
destructive, and "The Ballad of the Rattlesnake" symbolically relates this belief.

The iambic and anapestic dimeter quatrains contain vivid
imagery wrought in unforgettable detail. The senses respond to
the gripping narrative as the naked white man—staked, spit upon,
and gibbering with terror—watches the rattler writhe, coil, and
lurch at his face. Figurative language is used skillfully as the
similes, metaphors, and personification illustrate: the Apaches
laugh "like a frozen wind/In a crib of chaff"; the blond man lies
"like a bar of lead"; "Eternity ticks" behind his eyes; the desert
holds "in its frying-pan/The bones of a snake/And the bones of a
man." Unity, simplicity of narrative, connotative detail, and sym-

bolism characterize the ballad, which has appeal for many admirers of Tolson's work.

IV   *"A Hamlet Rives Us"*

Arthur E. Burke wrote of the poems in *Rendezvous:* "He [Tolson] has the knack of epitomizing the significant experiences of man and of making these throb with well-controlled drama. . . . This suggests that his genius lies in the dramatic and lyrical veins. . . ." Burke does criticize, however, Tolson's inability to achieve "sufficient flexibility" in his Shakespearian sonnets, pointing out that "In form he is mechanical, in matter graphically succinct, and never obscure." [15] One poem in this group, "A Hamlet Rives Us," succeeds in sweeping the reader along with the protagonist, who searches in vain for the words to say to a friend suffering bereavement:

> I saw him faltering toward me in the street:
> His eyes emptied of living, his grief unshed.
> Pain pitted my heart and meshed my doubtful feet,
> As memory's alcove revealed his loved one dead.
>
> Our sorrows mated then, for I had lost
> The next of kin in the fogland of the year.
> And yet a Hamlet rives us when the frost
> Of death comes like a specter buccaneer.
>
> *I must console him in this awful hour:*
> *It is the wise and decent thing to do.*
> Embarrassed, helpless, I was thieved of power
> To utter the tags tragedy ordained untrue.
>
> My friend passed by, unseeing in his grief;
> And the lash of conscience gave me sweet relief.
> (63)

The literary allusion is the mark of much of Tolson's poetry. The line "a Hamlet rives us when the frost/Of death comes like a specter buccaneer" and others of its quality prompted critic Margaret Walker, winner of the 1942 Yale Poetry Award, to comment about the "arresting images" in *Rendezvous*.[16]

V *"The Town Fathers"*

Although the poems in *Rendezvous* explore many subjects, most of them either center on or refer to the prejudice with which the black American has had to contend for generations. Tolson knew well the danger a minority poet faces in dealing with the subject of race, and he accepted the challenge: "If a poet puts a social, political, or religious idea in his poem, the critic has a right to test its maturity or validity, just as I have a right to pass judgment on the material a carpenter uses. But no one has a right to tell the poet what idea to use." [17]

A poem which typifies Tolson's approach to racial discrimination is "The Town Fathers." This poem derived from his experiences as a resident of South Texas, where he saw the sign of which the poem tells. The irony, understatement, humor, and characterization of these lines make clear the difference between propaganda and poetry:

> At the Courthouse Square
> On the Fourth of July,
> Beneath Old Glory's
> Pyrotechnic sky,
> The town fathers met,
> Minus Bible and rye.
>
> Against the statue
> Of Confederate dead
> The Mayor spat
> His snuff and said,
> "We need a slogan!"
> And he palmed his head.
>
> The Sheriff's idioms
> Dynamited assent.
> The Judge croaked a phrase
> Latinistically bent.
> And the Mayor pondered
> With official intent.
>
> On a neon billboard,
> As high as a steeple,

The travelers puzzle
The amazing sequel:
*The Blackest Land
And the Whitest People.*
(22)

VI   *Reviews of* Rendezvous with America

At least two reviewers of *Rendezvous with America* pointed out
the differences between Tolson and other black poets, particularly
Paul Laurence Dunbar, whose poetry Tolson had recited "all over
Iowa" as a schoolboy and whose work he had imitated as a young
poet. Nathaniel Tillman wrote that "Much of the promise indicated in the best of the formal English poems of Dunbar reaches
its fulfillment in the poetry of Professor Tolson." [18] A Pittsburgh
Courier review said that Dunbar and Tolson are "as unlike as
Edgar Guest and Archibald MacLeish. Tolson is a significant intellect, a multicultured citizen of the world. He is a Shostakovich
in verse. He has mastered a new way of saying things. His are
glittering concentrates of passion and sense in new-fashioned ver-
bal habiliments." [19] The black novelist Richard Wright, whom Tolson admired greatly, wrote that "Tolson's poetic lines and images
sing, affirm, reject, predict, and judge. His vision is informed by
the core of Negro experience in America, and his poetry is direct
and humanistic. All history, from Genesis to Munich, is his domain." [20] His former student at Wiley College, James Farmer,
hailed him as "the dark Whitman." [21] Margaret Walker, former
editor of *Common Ground* and a poet-critic, evaluated him as "a
poet to be reckoned with by all poets." [22]

Good reviews outside the black press included Robert Hillyer's
statement in the New York *Times Book Review* that Tolson is "a
good poet and a good craftsman" whose versification is "unusually
deft." [23] Of *Rendezvous*, William Rose Benét commented in *Saturday Review:* "Mr. Tolson's book is remarkable. . . . He not only
is an exemplar of the finest qualities of his race, but a poet of
powerful rhythm and original language. You have only to begin
that remarkable poem, 'The Bard of Addis Ababa': 'Out of the
green glooms of Dambassa/Trots the massive yellow dog,/His
prowlike jaws, his forehead/Scarred like an axman's log,/His
growls presaging a menace/Like a fog-horn in a fog.' " [24]

Such comments could have been heady wine for the heretofore unrecognized poet, but Tolson was not one to rest content for long. He knew that a new school of poetry had emerged and gained acceptance among readers after having been accepted by poets for several years. He had followed with interest the increasing popularity of those poets who were the acknowledged spokesmen for the New Poetry: Pound, Eliot, Yeats, and—though his technique differed markedly from the others—Frost. Many of the poems in *Rendezvous* reflect the influence of earlier poets—Tillman named Whitman and Stephen Vincent Benét, to mention only two—but Tolson's interest in experimentation is also evident. Along with James Joyce and the early William Butler Yeats, he shared a liking for "hypnotic undulations of language." [25] He used many literary and historical allusions, displaying special learning in diverse areas much as did Pound and Eliot, particularly in their earlier work. Many of his characters are common folk, akin to Frost's New Englanders; and the poems frequently express a homespun philosophy with Frostian whimsy and wit. The road which Tolson was taking is indicated clearly in his notes for a speech that he was preparing some five years after the publication of *Rendezvous* to give at a small college for black students in Kentucky:

Now the time has come for a New Negro Poetry for the New Negro. The most difficult thing to do today is to write modern poetry. Why? It is the acme of the intellectual. Longfellow, Whittier, Milton, Tennyson, and Poe are no longer the poets held in high repute. The standard of poetry has changed completely. Negroes must become aware of this. This is the age of T. S. Eliot who just won the Nobel Prize in Literature.[26] If you know Shakespeare from A to Z, it does not mean you can read one line of T. S. Eliot! . . . Imitation must be in technique only. We have a rich heritage of folk lore and history. We are a part of America. We are a part of the world. Our native symbols must be lifted into the universal. Yes, we must study the techniques of Robert Lowell, Dylan Thomas, Carlos Williams, Ezra Pound, Karl Shapiro, W. H. Auden. The greatest revolution has not been in science but in poetry. We must study such magazines as *Partisan Review*, the *Sewanee Review, Accent,* and the *Virginia Quarterly.* We must read such critics as Crowe Ransom, Allen Tate, Stephen Spender, George Dillon and Kenneth Burke.

These observations reveal the attitude which was the shaping force of the technique that emerges in Tolson's *Libretto for the Republic of Liberia* in 1953. *Rendezvous,* he realized, was not the work which would establish a niche for him in American litera-ture. On the back of an envelope among his notes is scribbled this description of a poet:

> Not satisfied
>   with fire, water, earth, and air,
>   the poet seeks a fifth essence on
>   the astral stair.

CHAPTER 3

Libretto for the Republic of Liberia

"Africa is a rubber ball;
the harder you dash it to the ground,
the higher it will rise."
—Tolson, *Libretto*

IN 1947, the Liberian government commissioned Tolson to be poet laureate of Liberia, the result of another Hardeian "artistry of circumstance." When he was teaching in Marshall, Texas, one of his male students had dropped by with his girl friend one evening to chat with the Tolsons; and the young woman had mentioned that she was related to someone in the Liberian embassy. Tolson never knew how he was selected to be the poet laureate of Liberia, but the only connection he had ever had with the African Republic was his former student's friend with whom he had talked briefly that one evening. After the invitation, Tolson immediately began work on a poem in honor of Liberia to celebrate the centennial of the founding of the little African republic; and he completed it within a year.

A letter from George Dillon, one of the editors of *Poetry* magazine, dated September 27, 1948, indicates that Tolson had submitted the poem to him for consideration. Dillon wrote Tolson that the poem was "a very good performance, much stronger than we would expect such an occasional poem to be." The members of the editorial staff suggested that the last stanza of the first section and the entire last section did not seem "good enough for the rest." They commended particularly the "new imagery," the "nice sense of disciplined rhythm," and the management of the "vivid and interesting" historical allusions. Dillon explained that, because they were overstocked with manuscripts at the time and because the poem was long, the three editors had not given his poem the unanimous vote necessary for publication.[1]

[72]

Tolson continued to work on the ode to Liberia. In 1950, *Poetry* magazine, edited by Karl Shapiro, featured one section of the *Libretto for the Republic of Liberia*. Dodd, Mead and Company, publishers of *Rendezvous with America,* refused to publish the occasional poem about an obscure little country; but Twayne Publishers published the book six years after Tolson's appointment as poet laureate of Liberia. Those six years mark one of the most important stages of Tolson's development as a "modern" poet.

I   *Influence of Allen Tate on Form of* Libretto

One person who exerted considerable influence on Tolson's technique at this time might have helped him determine his course stylistically thirty years earlier had circumstances been different. As a freshman at Fisk University in 1919, Tolson was just across the city from Vanderbilt University, where the leaders of the Fugitive group—Donald Davidson, John Crowe Ransom, Allen Tate, and Robert Penn Warren—were inaugurating the Southern literary renaissance. Several years later, through reading the "little magazines," Tolson became aware of the importance of the work of the sixteen poets[2] who had met frequently from 1915 to 1928 to read and discuss their work and to publish *The Fugitive,* a journal devoted primarily to their poetry. He often thought how fortunate he would have been had he participated in this creative-writing venture, which "precipitated quarrels, arguments, and experiments that caused a group of talented men to interact upon each other and, finally, to share in an experience of reality which has provided one of the major insights in modern literature."[3]

As it was, Tolson's introduction to the influential voices in twentieth-century poetry resulted not from any direction or interaction with other poets but from his intensive reading, which was slowly shaping his ideas about such poetry. The following year he ran across a copy of Carl Sandburg's "Chicago" in the university library, and his career as a poet came nearer to getting a real start. Unfortunately, he took the poem to one of his professors, who advised him strongly to "Leave that stuff alone . . . and go back to the Romantics and Victorians!" Had Tolson followed his own intuition, he would most likely have developed the style of his maturity much earlier. A few years later, however, when he picked up a copy of Eliot's *The Waste Land* in a New York bookstore, he knew that his course lay ahead rather than with the past.

Eventually, Tolson found his way to the mainstream of modern poetry, but the journey of the solitary student was a long and tedious one. Now, three decades after he had unknowingly crossed paths with the group of young poets in Nashville, Tennessee, he sent the manuscript of *Libretto* to Allen Tate, one of the original Fugitives and a leader in the New Poetry movement, with the request that he write a preface for it. After Tate read the manuscript, he returned it, saying that he was not interested in the propaganda of a Negro poet.[4] Tolson could have reacted with bitterness to the southerner's blunt rejection, claiming that Tate was prejudiced. Instead, Tolson told himself that an astute critic had pinpointed a weakness which he himself had often criticized in the work of black poets. During the next year, he concentrated, therefore, on the style of modern poets and revised his technique in *Libretto*. Guided by his "three S's of Parnassus," he turned the propaganda which Tate had found offensive into symbols and into far-ranging literary and historical allusions. Then he sent the *Libretto* back to him.

The preface which Allen Tate wrote for the *Libretto for the Republic of Liberia* states, in part, that "there is a first-rate intelligence at work in this poem from first to last. . . . For the first time, it seems to me, a Negro poet has assimilated completely the full poetic language of his time, and, by implication, the language of the Anglo-American poetic tradition." [5] Tate's endorsement was quite an accomplishment for the little-known poet. At the same time, Tolson could not resist chuckling as he pointed out to Mrs. Tolson parallel passages in his original manuscript and in the revised *Libretto*. Tate's earlier objection to the poem had made clear to Tolson that in technique lay the answer to the dilemma which plagued him as an Afro-American poet whose integrity demanded that he be true both to his heritage and to the standard of artistic excellence.

Tate's evaluation of Tolson affirms that the poet had satisfied the critic's requirement of making "the main thing . . . the poetry, if one is a poet, whatever one's color may be" and, in universalizing the black man's experiences. Tate wrote in his preface his view of Tolson as an "intensely Negro" poet:

I think that Mr. Tolson has assumed this [that the "main thing" is the poetry]; and the assumption, I gather, has made him not less but more intensely *Negro* in his apprehension of the world than any of his contemporaries, or any that I have read. But by becoming more intensely Negro he seems to me to dismiss the entire problem, so far as poetry is concerned, by putting it in its properly subordinate place. In the end I found I was reading *Libretto for the Republic of Liberia* not because Mr. Tolson is a Negro but because he is a poet, not because the poem has a "Negro subject" but because it is about the world of all men. And this subject is not merely asserted; it is embodied in a rich and complex language and realized in terms of the poetic imagination.[6]

Tolson had always said that to emphasize the *how* does not deemphasize the *what*. He stressed both the *how* and the *what* in his revision of *Libretto*. In this way, his work won the commendation of the influential critic[7] without diminishing the strength of his message about the inspirational story of Liberia.

II   *Content and Form of* Libretto

The *Libretto* is a long ode consisting of eight sections named for the diatonic scale: "Do," "Re," "Mi," "Fa," "Sol," "La," "Ti," "Do." The poem opens with the question *Liberia?*, and the remaining 769 lines provide the answer. Although the poem specifically concerns the nation of Liberia, it pursues some of the themes treated in *Rendezvous with America:* racial prejudice, exploitation of the black man by the white man, and the accusation of Gertrude Stein that the Negro "suffers from Nothingness," themes which continue in *Harlem Gallery.* In *Libretto*, even more than in the later *Harlem Gallery,*

> Idea and image,
> form and content,
> blend like pigment with pigment
> in a flesh color.[8]

The themes and the sociological and philosophical beliefs of the poet did not change in the nine-year interval between *Rendezvous* and *Libretto*, but stylistic effects which were developing in *Ren-*

dezvous—allusions, symbolism, the metaphor, the "three S's of Parnassus"—now assume in *Libretto* a major role; and an additional concept of form emerges in it as the spine of the work. Tolson looked upon Hart Crane's *The Bridge* as the greatest modern ode of the English language, but he felt it had failed. To avoid this pitfall, he had to come to a full understanding of *climax*, a partial meaning of which had escaped him through the years. As he planned his ode, he thought long about climax; and he recalled suddenly that the word was a derivative of the Greek word meaning *ladder*. For the first time, the concept was clear to him: the poet snares the reader's interest on the first rung of the ladder; each rung is one step higher; but all are essential. When the poet steps on the bottom rung and looks up, he may not know what the seventh rung will be. He is like a man in a tunnel who sees the light at the end—it may be flashlight or moonlight; he cannot tell until he moves closer to it.[9]

With this revelation in mind, Tolson conceived the plan for *Libretto* in which each of the eight sections, which would be named for the notes of the scale, would be a rung on the ladder, constituting the climax. Out of metrical diversity would come originality of form. His "three-S" formula would light the way, and his thorough grounding in grammar would help to keep him from stumbling stylistically.

III   *"Do"*

The initial "Do" section of *Libretto* consists of seven similarly constructed eight-line stanzas. The first line of each is the italicized question *Liberia?* The centered, balanced lines capture the eye.

Liberia?
No micro-footnote in a bunioned book
Homed by a pedant
With a gelded look:
You are
The ladder of survival dawn men saw
In the quicksilver sparrow that slips
The eagle's claw!

(ll. 1–8)

Various critics have commented on the felicity of the concluding symbol in this stanza. In an article entitled "The Quicksilver Sparrow of M. B. Tolson," Dan McCall speaks of the "extraordinary beauty of the opening image." [10] Even Tate admits, "On the first page I received a shock in that region where bored scepticism awaits the new manuscript from a poet not clearly identified, when I saw Liberia invoked as '. . . the quicksilver sparrow that slips/The eagle's claw!' " [11]

To understand the full implication of the metaphor, it is necessary to know something of the history of Liberia in order to learn how the Liberian "quicksilver" sparrow slipped the claw of the American eagle. Charles Morrow Wilson, in his history of Liberia (1947), states that long before 1776 many Americans considered slavery immoral; and Samuel Hopkins had published in Boston three years before the American Revolution a plan for training freed slaves as colonizers and missionaries for Africa. The slave trade continued, however; and, as the number of freed Negroes grew, the problem of the "unkept Africans" began to get out of hand.

In 1818 the American Colonization Society, instituted by missionary groups and semiformally adopted by the legislatures of Maryland and Virginia, dispatched a ship and committee to negotiate for a colony site near Sierra Leone. The next year President James Monroe officially approved the purchase from natives of Sherbro Island of a promontory which was to be the Liberian coast. Congress appropriated federal funds to "colonize and build huts for recaptured slaves and to provide the latter with farming utensils, teachers, arms, and ammunition." On February 6, 1820, the *Elizabeth* sailed from Philadelphia with eighty-six freed slaves aboard. At Sherbro Island, the group learned that the tribesmen would not sell the island site. After a siege of illness on shipboard which claimed thirty-one lives, the survivors were put ashore at the British settlement near Freetown in Sierra Leone.

The next year the society purchased a strip of land one hundred and thirty miles long and forty miles deep to be used for the settlement of American freed slaves. The little colony survived trials by hunger, fever, and native attacks. In 1822, a young clergyman, Jehudi Ashmun, and his wife sailed on the brig *Strong* with thirty-seven freed Afro-Americans for the newly founded commonwealth. When they arrived a few months later, they found that over one-third of the original settlers had died and that the others were ill. Native tribes were planning an attack on the survivors. Ashmun's wife died shortly after their arrival; though grief-stricken, he nevertheless directed the men in fortifying the settlement; and, when nine hundred tribesmen overran the camp in November, they were turned back repeatedly by the United States Navy cannon manned by Ashmun. After three weeks, the natives retired, leaving the ailing colonists to clear land, build fences, and plant crops. Ashmun remained in Liberia until 1828, when he returned to the United States and died a few days later at the age of thirty-five. Somehow, the commonwealth survived jungle disease, hunger, and attacks of hostile natives. On July 26, 1847, it established a constitutional government similar to that of the United States and became the Republic of Liberia.

England and France continued to make claims on Liberian lands, and between 1847 and 1910 Liberia lost 44 percent of her land. At this time, the United States recognized its moral commitment to the lone African republic and offered assistance in such areas as education, finance, military training, agronomy, and medicine. Since then, Liberia has proved her worth to the United States and to the world. In 1918 she joined the Allies, and she was providing at least 97 percent of the rubber in use by the end of World War I and had established essential airfields and harbors for the Allies.[12] Not only had she "slipped the eagle's claw," but she had assisted the eagle to fly.

Tolson was pleased with the quicksilver sparrow image, and he sometimes used it in class to illustrate how the symbol originates with the poet. He moves horizontally from the fact to the metaphor; then the idea moves vertically from the metaphor to the symbol at the apex of the angle:

Symbol   (C)

Metaphor   (B) ← (A)   Historical fact

In the *Libretto*, the metaphor is the vehicle on which the opening section moves. Following the question *Liberia?* which opens each stanza, lines two, three, and four state metaphorically what Liberia

is *not:* "No side-show barker's bio-accident"; "No oil-boiled Barab-
bas"; "No pimple on the chin of Africa"; "No Cobra Pirate of the
Question Mark"; "No waste land yet, nor yet a destooled elite."
The last four lines of each stanza affirm what Liberia *is:* a glorious
republic of free men descended from a few disease-ridden ex-
slaves cast on the shores of a hostile continent. Liberia is "the
ladder of survival dawn"; "the lightning rod of Europe, Canaan's
key"; "*Libertas* flayed and naked by the road/To Jericho"; "Black
Lazarus risen from the White Man's grave"; "American genius un-
crowned in Europe's charnel house." "Do" ends with the pro-
nouncement:

> You are
> The iron nerve of lame and halt and blind,
> Liberia and not Liberia,
> A moment of the conscience of mankind!
> (ll. 53 56)

Forcefulness and strength are effected in these lines in which
content and form blend, guided by the "three S's." The centered
lines of varied length are unified by the pattern: the initial *Liberia?*, the metaphors of negation, and the metaphors of affir-
mation. Varied line length combines with an *abcbdefe* rhyme
scheme. Figurative language and imagery are prominent. In the
opening stanza alliterative phrases such as "*B*unioned *b*ook" and
"*s*urvival dawn men *s*aw/In the quicksilver *s*parrow that *s*lips" are
frequent. Onomatopoetic effects abound, as does assonance, in
such groups of words as "micr*o*-fo*o*tn*o*te," "h*o*ned"; "fo*o*tn*o*te,"
"b*oo*k," "l*oo*k"; "d*aw*n," "s*aw*," "cl*aw*"; and "qui*c*ksi*l*ver," "s*l*ips."
The average reader encounters two problems in the opening
lines, and these problems increase with each page. As one critic
points out, "the *Libretto* is immensely difficult—obscure and ref-
erential, composed in several languages and buttressed with now-
scholarly, now-sly notes to historiography, anthropology, philosophy, music, odd-lore." [13] An additional problem is understanding
the allusions after the reader has tracked them down. The first
problem is more difficult than the second, however; for, when one
knows the source of the allusion and understands its context in the
poem, the meaning is usually clear. For this reason, Tolson said

that he did not regard his work as esoteric; but he did agree before *Libretto*'s publication to add a seventeen-page section of notes.

Tolson's style in *Libretto* was not an affirmative answer to the plea of Stéphane Mallarmé to ignore the masses: "Oh, poets, you have always been proud; now be more than proud, be scornful!" [14] Tolson was neither a scornful person nor a scornful poet, but he did refuse to "write down." Prejudiced at first against modern poetry, he came to believe that "a poet works on a poem as a mathematician works on a problem"—that a first-rate poem does not yield itself totally to the reader on the first reading.[15] He had mastered traditional form, and he now used it as a basis for his experiments with a new form, even perhaps a new language. His language is reminiscent of the new one that Arthur Rimbaud called upon poets to produce—a language "of the soul, for the soul, containing everything, smells, sounds, colours; thought latching on to thought and pulling. The poet would define the amount of the unknown awakening in the universal soul in his own time: he would produce more than the formulation of his thought or the measurement *of his march towards Progress!* . . . Eternal art will have its function, since poets are citizens. Poetry will no longer rhyme with action: *it will be ahead of it!*" [16]

Anyone who reads the predictions in the concluding sections of *Libretto* and recalls that the prophecies were made when Liberia was one of only two republics in Africa cannot but feel that the poem was ahead of its time. Moreover, both John Ciardi and Karl Shapiro express this belief in their criticism. Though Shapiro claims that "the forms of the *Libretto* and of *Harlem Gallery* . . . are the Negro satire upon the poetic tradition of the Eliots and Tates," [17] it seems more likely that Tolson was interested in writing ably on his subject in the style in which he believed the best modern poems were being written and in which he could best express himself artistically—a style which appealed to him greatly because of his love of words; his extensive knowledge of literature, history, and philosophy; his interest in grammar; and his desire to communicate his beliefs without being didactic. Tolson, as has been noted, spent years analyzing and absorbing the techniques of Pound, Eliot, and other "great Moderns";[18] and their influence has been noted by most critics of his work, particularly in the far-ranging allusions which make necessary the section of notes, though Tolson is ever the black poet in terms of the content of his work.

Even after consulting the notes section, a conscientious reader keeps an unabridged dictionary close at hand. The first note, for instance, directs the reader to the source of the sparrow-eagle image—Dryden's *All For Love*, II, i: "upon my eagle's wings/I bore this wren, till I was tired of soaring,/and now he mounts above me." To grasp the full connotation of the image, the reader must understand both Dryden's figurative lines and the history of the founding of Liberia, as well as the juxtaposition of the two. Many of the other notes are even less helpful. The line "No corpse of a soul's errand" (l. 11) is noted simply "Cf. Raleigh, *The Soul's Errand.*" Tolson intended *Libretto* to be a challenge, even to the intellectual. Though certainly not his major objective, one intention was to show that he could play well the modern poetry game. He told one puzzled reader of the *Libretto:* "My friend, it took me six years to write it. Is it surprising that it takes more than one reading to understand it?" More important, however, was his desire to create a work of art which would stand as a monument to Liberians and to black men everywhere who have traversed the road from adversity to achievement.

IV "*Re*"

Following the glorification of Liberia in "Do," the "Re" section describes and defines the republic "before/America set the raw foundling on Africa's/Doorstep . . ." (ll. 59–61). It consists of ten sections of irregular verse, and parts one, four, seven, and ten are irregular couplets. The unifying device of repetition is continued here; the first line of each couplet is "The Good Gray Bard in Timbuktu chanted," and the second lines are African proverbs, the first two in native dialect. The first line of the concluding couplet employs emphatic variation as it changes from "The Good Gray Bard in Timbuktu chanted" to "The Good Gray Bard *chants no longer in Timbuktu.*" The six, six-line stanzas are not centered, as in "Do"; but balance and repetition are secured by the pattern of the number of lines in the stanzas: 2442442442. Parallel construction appears in several lines as well as within some of the lines.

"Re" describes the kingdom of Songhai ("Before Liberia was,

Songhai was"), which flourished when Black Askia, an African king who had ruled a territory larger than Europe for twenty-four years, "gave the Bengal light/Of Books the Inn of Court in Songhai . . ." (ll. 74–75). Black youths studied at the great University of Sankoré, where "Footloose professors, chimney sweeps of the skull/From Europe and Asia," "white scholars like El-Akit," and "Black humanists like Bagayogo" made them welcome: "*Karibu wee!*" Then the Portuguese, the Spanish, and the Arabs razed the African empire. The elements of sound and sense are effective in the last two stanzas of "Re," which pictures the country after the savage attacks:

> And now the hyenas whine among the barren bones
> Of the seventeen sun sultans of Songhai,
> And hooded cobras, hoodless mambas, hiss
> In the gold caverns of Falémé and Bambuk,
> And puff adders, hook scorpions, whisper
> In the weedy corridors of Sankoré. *Lia! Lia!*
>
> The Good Gray Bard chants no longer in Timbuktu:
> "The maggots fat on yeas and nays of nut empires!"
> (ll. 93–100)

Tolson liked the sound of these lines. He enjoyed telling about quoting the line "seventeen sun sultans of Songhai" to Peter Viereck, who had stated at a reception in the Liberian embassy honoring the poet laureate that there cannot be more than three instances of alliteration or assonance in a line of poetry. These lines are alive not only with alliterative phrases but also with assonance and onomatopoeia. A line laden with both alliteration and assonance in this section is "The Good Gray Bard in Timbuktu chanted."

Powerful imagery marks this stanza: the ear hears, the eye sees, and the blood chills as the hyenas whine among the skeletons, the cobras and mambas hiss in the caverns, and the puff adders and scorpions whisper in the weedy corridors. The names *Songhai, Falémé, Bambuk,* and *Sankoré* are romantic in their appeal to the imagination, enhancing the mystery of the far away. There are many striking images in "Re," such as "Burnt warriors and watermen of Songhai/Tore in *bizarreries* the uniforms of Portugal/And sewed an imperial quilt of tribes" (ll. 62–64); "Europe bartered

Africa crucifixes for red ivory,/Gewgaws for black pearls, *pierres d'aigris* for green gold" (ll. 68–70); "And the leopard Saracen bolted his scimitar into/The jugular vein of Timbuktu . . ." (ll. 91–92).

The author's notes identify eleven allusions in "Re." The forty-three lines encompass history, literature, and several languages as they move from Pliny to Sagittarius, from Shakespeare to W. E. B. DuBois, from the African proverb *"Wanawake wanazaa ovyo! Kazi yenu wazungu!"* (The women keep having children right and left. 'Tis the work of you white men!") to the French pro-nouncement *"Dieu seul est grand,"* which, according to Tolson's notes at the end of the poem, were the first words of Jean Baptiste Massillon's exordium, delivered at the magnificent funeral of Louis XIV, which brought the congregation to its feet in the ca-thedral.

V *"Mi"*

"Mi" takes up the original plan of American church leaders and others to send some of the freed slaves to Africa. The poet names and characterizes metaphorically, in a word or phrase, various Americans who took some part in making the arrangements. Rob-ert Finley, "Jehovah's Damasias," played a major role as one of the instigators of the movement to return the ex-slaves to Africa. He "swooped into Pennsylvania Avenue/To pinion" Henry Clay, the "shuttlecock," [19] and Bushrod Washington, both of whom served as early presidents of the American Colonization Society. Finley's "magnet yea" also attracted the support of such men as Francis Scott Key, "the hymnist primed to match a frigate's guns"; the influential Bishop Meade, "God's purse"; and antislavery re-former Charles Turner Torrey, "the People's clock," a minister who later became a martyr in the cause of Abolition. [20]

Together, these men worked to effect the decision which "verved/Black Pilgrim Fathers to Cape Mesurado." The verb *verved* is one of several instances in which the poet seems to have been captivated by the sound of the word, resulting in a phrase which is hardly inevitable. The poet notes that "That decision's cash/And credit bought a balm for conscience" (ll. 114–15). Al-though the objectives of the society were ostensibly to introduce Christianity and to promote civilization in Africa, one major incentive was to relieve the slaveholding states from the inconvenience of an increase of free blacks. Little did either the white sponsors or the black colonists dream that one day the descendants of the superfluous ex-slaves would assist the United States in winning a war.

The free-verse pattern of "Re" is exchanged in "Mi" for six, four-line stanzas of iambic pentameter, unrhymed except for lines two and three in the first stanza. The concluding five lines, italicized for emphasis, draw a sharp contrast between the rather muddled beginning of the struggling colony and the vital role Liberia played in both world wars by providing, as has been noted, rubber for the Allies and, in World War II, airfields from which seventeen thousand bombers a month flew against General Rommel's *Afrika Korps*.

> No linguist of the Braille of prophecy ventured:
> *The rubber from Liberia shall arm*
>
> *Free peoples and her airport hinterlands*
> *Let loose the winging grapes of wrath upon*
> *The Desert Fox's cocained nietzscheans*
> *A goosestep from the Gateway of the East!*
>   (ll. 119–24)

Lines from "The Battle Hymn of the Republic"—"He is trampling out the vintage where the *grapes of wrath* are stored/He hath *loosed* the fateful lightning of His terrible swift sword"—are juxtaposed with the Liberian story to read: "Let *loose* the winging *grapes of wrath*." The participle *winging* makes the bombs dropped from the airplanes the modern-day "terrible swift sword."

Sound is emphasized in these lines through the use of alliteration, onomatopoeia, and assonance. In the two concluding lines, the penultimate line is strained in contrast to the smooth final line. Cacophonous initial sounds stress the ugliness of the situation in imagery which is strained both in idea and in sound: *"The Desert Fox's cocained nietzscheans/A goosestep from the Gateway of the East!"* Besides sound, the sense element is equally stressed in this section. Aware that one of the tests of a poet is his usage of nouns, verbs, and adjectives, Tolson uses *hinterlands* to convey the feeling of Liberia's isolation. He makes the noun *airport* an adjective—"airport hinterlands" in the war. The alliterative phrase "let loose" is expelled with the force of the arrow it calls to mind. The participle *winging* intensifies the image. "Grapes of wrath" carries the full connotation of its context in "Battle Hymn of the Republic" and in Steinbeck's novel. Rommel's nickname "Desert Fox" is connotative of a sly animality or bestiality. "Cocained" is forceful, and "goosestep" conjures up the image of the march of the Führer's fanatic followers, though the poet can be seen too obviously at work in this phrase and in the concluding hyperbole: *"A goosestep from the Gateway of the East."*

VI   *"Fa"*

The short "Fa" section is Tolson at his best, and it was one of the parts of *Libretto* that he enjoyed reading to audiences and talking about. Composed of three striking symbols of predator nations which attack the young republic, then rest in preparation for future attacks, the image-packed section illustrates the synchronization of sight, sound, and sense:

> A fabulous mosaic log,
> The Bola boa lies
> gorged to the hinges of his jaws,
> eyeless, yet with eyes . . .
>
> *in the interlude of peace.*
>
> The beaked and pouched assassin sags
> on to his corsair rock,
> and from his talons swim the blood-
> red feathers of a cock . . .
>
> *in the interlude of peace.*
>
> The tawny typhoon striped with black
> torpors in grasses tan:
> a doomsday cross, his paws uprear
> the leveled skull of a man . . .
>
> *in the interlude of peace.*
>   (ll. 125–39)

Selden Rodman says of these lines that the "lyric passages" are as "subtle as they are incisive." [21] The poet's artistry reveals itself in the spacing and placement of the lines; in the parallelism of the symbols and of the choral line, which pauses just as the predators pause "in the interlude of peace"; and in the color which heightens the connotation of the images: the "mosaic" log, the "blood-red" feathers which "swim" from the assassin's talons, the "tawny typhoon striped with black" which "torpors in grasses tan."

The section builds from the unnamed victim of the snake to the cock killed by his fellow to man, whose "leveled skull" is mauled by a marauding tiger. Each predator rests between attacks: the boa lies gorged; the assassin cock sags onto a rock; the tiger "torpors" in the grass. The lines are rich with poetic devices; and, read aloud, the section illustrates the work of both artist and musician. When Stanley Hyman recognized Tolson's technique of juxtaposition as having kinship to the associative organization of the blues, Tolson was at first surprised. He had intended the poem to be quite literary; but, when he studied it carefully, he also discovered the syncopation and counterpoint which he had unconsciously incorporated into the poem.[22]

In Tolson's lecture at Langston University during Fine Arts Week in April, 1965, the poet recalled the sources of the metaphors and symbols in the first stanza. Somewhere in his reading he had stumbled across that "wonderfully alliterative name the *Bola Boa.*" Then he had read a book about some young men traveling in Africa who had sat on what they thought was a log—until it moved. Always interested in animals (Tolson sometimes told his audiences that he visited the zoo to learn more about *them*), he was particularly fascinated by snakes; and many allusions to them appear in his poetry. *Mosaic* seemed to him to describe the appearance of the boa, and he had selected "the best of all possible adjectives" to describe the boa—"fabulous." He demonstrated that one cannot say *fabulous* without opening wide both his mouth and his eyes—a most appropriate facial expression. "Gorged" was more connotative than its synonym, "full," while "hinges of his jaws" was simply an accurate biological description.

Tolson also warned his audience in the Fine Arts Week lecture to watch for the "subterranean" meaning in his work. For in-

stance, "Europe is an empty python in hiding grass" is not a statement about pythons, he pointed out, nor even a *python,* but about
a python. The symbol of exploitation, the python devours, rests,
and devours again. Tolson went ahead in his lecture to elaborate
on symbolism as a trait of Negro spirituals as well as of modern
poetry. When the black man sang "Steal Away to Jesus," he was
planning on using the underground railroad for transportation.
Other characteristics which modern poetry and Negro spirituals
share, he pointed out, include figurative language and juxtaposition of biblical and folk materials which exhibit humor, satire, and
pathos.

Tolson's manipulation of symbolism, alliteration, assonance,
and onomatopoeia enrich the "Fa" section. The meter and rhyme
also enhance the effectiveness of the sound, while Tolson achieves
tone variation by changing from the aggressive active in each
stanza to the subdued passive in the ironic choral line *"in the interlude of peace."*

VII *"Sol"*

"Sol" is the most interesting section of the *Libretto* to many
readers because of the mixture of humor, irony, and wisdom in
the thirty African proverbs it contains. The section begins by
introducing the "horned American dilemma"—what to do with
the freed black slaves—a dilemma which white Americans sought
to solve by readying to sail to Africa the brig *Elizabeth,* which

> . . . flaunts her stern
> At auction blocks with the eyes of Cain
> And down-the-river sjamboks.
>   (ll. 146–48)

Soon the ship crosses the Middle Passage, where "the sharks wax
fattest and the stench/Goads God to hold his nose!" (ll.153–54).
Elijah Johnson, courageous black leader of the colonists, wonders,
"How long? How long? How long?"

The middle section of "Sol" consists of the proverbs, handed
down through the centuries by the tribal *Griot,* the walking encyclopedia who carried in his head the legends and lore of his
people. Most of the proverbs which appear in this section are in

the form in which they were conceived.[23] Several of them, which Tolson described as "intelligence working on experience," have racial implications:

> "Africa is a rubber ball;
> the harder you dash it to the ground,
> the higher it will rise.
> > (ll. 173–75)

> ". . . God saves the black
> man's soul but not his buttocks from
> the white man's lash. . . .
> > (ll. 200–202)

> ". . . The white man solves
> between white sheets his black

> "problem. Where would the rich cream be
> without skim milk? . . ."
> > (ll. 207–10)

Such sayings, he emphasized, refute Gertrude Stein's charge that the Negro suffers from Nothingness.

The section closes with Elijah Johnson musing on the outcome of the venture in Liberia which had taken so many lives; but the alternative—slavery—is worse, no matter what the odds. The "benediction" of the poet, as he raises the Liberian story into the universal, is

> And every ark awaits its raven,
> Its vesper dove with an olive-leaf,
> Its rainbow over Ararat.
> > (ll. 224–26)

The form of "Sol" differs from that of the preceding sections. As the excerpts demonstrate, it consists of twenty-nine unrhymed three-line stanzas. Lines one and two are predominantly iambic tetrameter; line three, iambic trimeter. There is much symbolism and figurative language, particularly in the proverbs. Phrases from Old Gaelic, French, and native African dialects appear in the section, which also contains many biblical allusions.

VIII *"La"*

In "La," which is composed of seven *abcb* iambic trimeter quatrains, the poet contrasts the primitive Africa with the land which Jehudi Ashmun, "a white man spined with dreams," who gave his life in establishing the settlement of freed black men against innumerable obstacles, helped to establish. The section ends with Ashmun's declaration:

> ". . . My Negro kinsmen,
> America is my mother,
> Liberia is my wife,
> And Africa my brother."
>   (ll. 251–54)

IX *"Ti"*

"Ti," one of the most difficult sections of the poem in terms of juxtaposition, condensation, and allusions to dozens of sources in several languages, opens with a five-line, centered stanza with an *abcdb* rhyme scheme; and the sixth line is the italicized biblical "Selah!" which concludes each stanza in the section. The twelve remaining stanzas consist of lines which exhibit rhyme and range from ten to twenty-seven lines in length. The initial stanza of "Ti" invokes the "Calendar of the Century" that it may "red-letter the Republic's birth" and grant protection to Liberia. The deceitful "blind men" stand between England and France, nations which no longer have the power to rend Liberia, "making the multitudinous seas incarnadine." The protagonist addresses the "Great White World," explaining that "omega hounds/lap up the alpha laugh" and the curse which covered all.

The third stanza opens by calling on Africa, "Mother of Science," admonishing her to remember her history:

> O Africa, Mother of Science
> . . . *lachen mit yastchekes* . . .
> What dread hand
> to make tripartite one august event
> sundered Gondwanaland?
> What dread grasp crushed your biceps and

> back upon the rack
> chaos of chance and change
> fouled in Malebolgean isolation?
> What dread *elboga* shoved your soul
> into the *tribulum* of retardation?
> melamin or melanin dies to the world and dies:
> Rome casketed herself in Homeric hymns.
> Man's culture in barb and Arab lies:
> The Jordan flows into the Tiber,
> The Yangtze into the Thames,
> the Ganges into the Mississippi, the Niger
> into the Seine.
> Judge of the Nations, spare us: yet,
> fool latins, alumni of one school,
> on Clochan-na-n'all, say *Phew*
> . . . *Lest we forget! Lest we forget!* . . .
> to dusky peers of Roman, Greek, and Jew.
> *Selah!*
>
> (ll. 273–96)

The second line refers to the black man's courage in the face of pain or death—literally, he is laughing while needles are being stuck in him. Stanley Hyman, who alludes to this line in *The Tangled Bush*, indicates that self-destructive humor, what the Germans call *"Galgen-humor,"* or gallows humor, is characteristic of all oppressed peoples.[24] The third and sixth lines recall William Blake's "The Tiger"; the "one august event" is a phrase lifted from Thomas Hardy's "The Convergence of the Twain," a poem which gives an ironic account of the luxury liner *Titanic,* which rammed an iceberg on her maiden voyage; and the stanza ends with the familiar lines from Rudyard Kipling's "Recessional"—*"Lest we forget! Lest we forget!"*

The poet's objective in referring to many literatures, many histories, many geographical locations, and many languages is to make the *Libretto* universal. John Ciardi, who is highly complimentary of Tolson's work, points out, however, that "There are times when Tolson's heaping on of image after image and of phrases from German, Spanish, French, and from African languages as well, leaves the reader knocked out: too much is happening too fast, and the result seems to be not exaltation but dizziness." [25] Such lines are these which take up the relationship of the poet to the masses. They exhibit internal rhyme and a play on the word *mass:*

"enmesh in ethos, in *masôreth,* the poet's flesh/intone the Mass of the class as the requiem of the mass . . ." (ll. 310–11). The section continues with the sardonic comment that the state, "helled in by Sancho's fears/of the bitter hug of the Great Fear, Not-To-Be" (ll. 331–32) has always hung the curtain—at times, an iron curtain. The one who doubts "the white book's colophon/is Truth's . . . wears the black flower T of doomed Laocoön" (ll. 338–40).

There have always been the two worlds of the many and the few, and Tolson's sympathy is with the many—though his audience is undoubtedly the Few. The age has such "kinks internal and global stinks" that the speaker would prefer to be a dog, a monkey, or a hog. It is indeed difficult for Africans, "Peoples of the Brinks," to have the wisdom to solve "the riddle of/the Red Enigma and the White Sphinx" (ll. 376–77). Just as Tolson lifts "Pasez" from the Hebrew (his note explains that this is a vertical line that occurs about four hundred and eighty times in the Bible and is the most mysterious sign in the literature), so he turns to Spanish—*el grito de Dolores*—to express the cry for freedom and to French to describe his disillusionment as a result of "poets, disemboweled" and "mulligan truth and lie"—*fiers instants promis à la faux* (proud moments promised to the scythe). The "little gray cattle," the peasants, cower before the predator twins pomp and power, the "Siamese wolves."

The next stanzas begin with parallel statements concerning the distance to the promised land for the masses, the *"Höhere"* or the height of spiritual achievement. "The *Höhere* of Gaea's children/is beyond the *dérèglement de tous les sens* . . ." (ll. 423–4). "The *Höhere* of X's children/is beyond Heralds' College . . ." (ll. 423–35). "Gaea's children," "God's step-children," and "X's children" are all "the Many," the masses. Their promised land is beyond the present-day world, beyond Rimbaud's "dislocation of the senses" or the "maggot democracy." Tolson pleads for all—*"En Masse/. . .* Christians, Jews, *ta ethne . . ."* (ll. 439–40). The Shakespearian image of the black Aethiop reaching at the sun is juxtaposed smoothly into stanza twelve with the description of the New African.

"Ti" concludes with a picture of the futility of the Many who will never chart and travel a course upward. Lists of names from various languages, along with metaphorical synonyms in English, verify the status of the poor in every land as they travel in circles, for they have no destination:

> . . . Today the mass,
> the Beast with a Maginot Line in its Brain,
> the staircase Avengers of base alloy,
> the *vile canaille—Gorii!*—the *Bastard-rasse,*
> the *uomo qualyque,* the *hoi barbaroi,*
> the *raya* in the *Oeil de Boeuf,*
> the *vsechelovek,* the *descamisados,* the *hoi polloi,*
> the Raw from the Coliseum of the Cooked,
> Il Duce's Whore, Vardaman's Hound—
> unparadised nobodies with maps of Nowhere
> ride the merry-go-round!
> *Selah!*
>
> (ll. 476–88)

X "Do"

The concluding section, "Do," has three sections. It begins with eleven, six-line, free-verse stanzas in which juxtaposition, allusions, phrases from foreign languages, and word concoctions are multiplied. The only punctuation marks are parentheses, hyphens, apostrophes, and periods following abbreviations; and there are no capital letters. Foreign phrases appear in every stanza. The lack of form symbolizes the turbulence, disorder, and hopelessness of Liberia during the Age of Exploitation: "the seven trumpets of today's baby boys[26] summon peace/and the walls come tumblin' down (Christ sleeps)" (ll. 547–48).

The poet has fun—partly at the reader's expense—with such stanzas as four, which poses the question "What is Man?":

> *vexilla regis prodeunt inferni* what is man f.r.a.i. *tò tí*
> (a professor of metaphysicotheologicocosmonigology
> a tooth puller a pataphysicist in a cloaca of error
> a belly's wolf a skull's tabernacle a #13 with stars
> a muses' darling a busie bee *de sac et de corde*
> a neighbor's bed-shaker a walking hospital on the walk)
>
> (ll. 508–12)

A part of the fun is the juxtaposition of elements foreign to one another—the pretentiousness of "professor of metaphysicotheo-

logicocosmonigology" (another Pangloss)[27] in close combination
with "a tooth puller" (also the nickname of the first martyr of
Brazilian independence), a "busie bee" followed by a foreign
phrase, and so on. Preceding the favorite question of Socrates, "*Tò
tí*," is "*f.r.a.i.*," a possible interpretation of which is "Fellow of the
Royal Anthropological Institute." Tolson's wit, his inclination to
spoof, and his extensive use of the metaphor are exhibited in such
phrases as "a pataphysicist in a cloaca of error"—the false
physicist is caught in a sewer of his own mistakes.

Whereas many of the phrases answering the question "What is
man?" have a surface meaning revealed through context and connotation (he is "a belly's wolf a skull's tabernacle a #13 with
stars"), most of these phrases have a deeper significance. A note
on this line reads, "510 *A belly's wolf*. Cf. Beaumont and Fletcher,
Woman Pleased." Also Malley: "Religion is a process of turning
your skull into a tabernacle, not of going up to Jerusalem once a
year." "*#13 with stars*: James Wilkinson, American general and
secret Spanish agent, who sought to establish an empire in the
Southwest under his own sword and sceptre."

One twenty-line, centered stanza which poses a series of questions about the future of Liberia separates the first section of "Do"
from the conclusion. These questions range from "Where is the
glory of the *mestizo* Pharaoh?" to "The black albatross about the
white man's neck?" The irony of the question is clear when one
recalls the opening statement of the book: Liberia is no "black
albatross about the white man's neck" but a "quicksilver sparrow"
which has slipped "the eagle's claw."

The first seven stanzas of the concluding section of "Do," in
which appear the prose paragraphs about which most critics of
Libretto have commented, several of them unfavorably, begin
with the phrase "The Futurafrique . . . ," symbol of the Liberia
of the future. Again the "S-Trinity" influences the appearance of
the line, the sound of the long vowels and the alliterative and onomatopoeic words, and the imagery of the poetic ride into the future:

> The Futurafrique strokes the thigh of Mount Bar-
>   clay and skis toward the Good-
>   lowe Straightaway, whose colo-
>   ratura sunset is the alpenglow

of cultures in the Shovelhead Era
of the Common Man . . .

(ll. 598–603)

Along with the numerous vowels which lengthen the sound in phrases denoting the sleek smoothness of the ride, one notices the number of initial *s*'s and *c*'s in the brief passage.

It is difficult to separate the sound from the sense as the imagery in these lines appeals to the senses of touch and sight primarily. The "Futurafrique" and "Mount Barclay" are personified as the *"chef d'oeuvre* of Liberian Motors . . . strokes the thigh of Mount Barclay" and "skis" toward the "Straightaway." There is joy in the verb play used to describe the journey of the Futurafrique: it *slips, slithers, escalades, idles, volplanes, zooms, zigzags, rockets, arcs, strokes, skis, glitters, vies, challenges, slices, rend* [s] *gut* [s]. The United Nations Limited, in the next four stanzas, *volts, careers, horseshoe curves, sheens, quakes, zoomzooms,* and *telescopes.* Then the "diesel-engined, fourfold-decked, swan-sleek" Bula Matadi *glides, swivels,* and *whirs.* Nor has the poet exhausted his stockpile of synonyms, for *"Le Premier des Noirs,* of Pan-African Airway" *whirs, meteors, waltzes, curvets,* and *eagles* through the Liberian skies. These verbs connote innumerable images of the Africa-to-be and lead to the final nine stanzas of "Do" and of the *Libretto.*

Allen Tate evaluates "Do" as "rhetorically effective" but as "not quite successful" poetry: "The last section begins in a six-line stanza which is controlled with considerable mastery, but the movement breaks down into Whitmanesque prose-paragraphs into which Mr. Tolson evidently felt he could toss all the loose ends of history, objurgation, and prophecy which the set theme seemed to require of him as official poet." Tate partially softens his criticism with the comment that "even this part of the poem is written with great energy" and that he points out this defect only because "the power and versatility of the other parts of the poem offset them" and demand close attention.[28]

The final section prophesies—in free verse, significantly—an Africa which only a visionary could imagine in 1953, an Africa over which today fly more than thirty free flags:

> The Parliament of African Peoples signets forever
> the *Recessional of Europe* and
> trumpets the abolition of itself:
> and no nation uses *Felis leo* or
> *Aquila heliaca* as the emblem
> of *blut und boden;* and the hyenas
> whine no more among the bar-
> ren bones of the seventeen sun-
> set sultans of Songhai; and the
> deserts that gave up the ghost
> to green pastures chant in the
> ears and teeth of the Dog, in
> the Rosh Hashana of the Afric
> calends: *"Honi soit qui mal y
> pense!"*
>
>   (ll. 756–70)

In this stanzaic finale, the poet picks up the symbols he used in "Re" and envisions a land in which hyenas whine no more among the "barren bones of the seventeen sunset sultans of Songhai," and the deserts transformed into green pastures "chant in the ears and teeth of the Dog: 'Shamed be he who thinks ill on it!' "

XI   *Reviews of Libretto*

Dan McCall points out that Tolson does not use the "learned allusivenesss" characteristic of earlier parts of the poem so much in "Do" but images native to Africa and ends with the celebration of scientific progress in Liberia, a new relationship in which "science imitates and works with the land, marries nature instead of violating her." Although McCall criticizes the final section for "looseness" and for lacking complete authority because the poet is not a native African, he observes that "Tolson has heralded the Recessional of Europe in terms of great sophistication and power. . . ." [29]

Of the concluding parts of the poem, Selden Rodman writes that "The stanzas of the later sections are composed of quotations, proverbs, invocations and clichés rendered in the language from which they are lifted and explicated (when it suits the author's fancy) in voluminous, pedantic notes." When Rodman compares

Tolson's style with that of Eliot, he notes that Tolson's taste is
"much more uneven." Rodman's criticism, like that of Tate, is
tempered by his admiration of the total work: "it is not only by all
odds the most considerable poem so far written by an American
Negro, but a work of poetic synthesis in the symbolic vein alto-
gether worthy to be discussed in the company of such poems as
'The Waste Land,' 'The Bridge,' and 'Paterson.' His poem opens
vistas undreamt of by the English-speaking poets of his race and
by few poets of other races." [30] An Australian critic says that Tolson's poetry "too obviously comes *via* Eliot and Pound." He finds
the "inner world of poetry, a story and rhythm" missing in the
Libretto, which instead consists of "encyclopedic erudition,
worldshaking utterances, sardonic epigrams. . . ." This commentary, one of the harsher criticisms of Tolson's work, states that
his poetry "comes boosted in public by a willing suspension of
critical disbelief among American reviewers towards a Negro who
has made the 'modern' grade in poetry" and that his poetry will
possibly never be assimilated, even by poets.[31]

   Tolson never replied publicly to these criticisms, but the rough
draft of a letter among his papers addressed to Cral Murphy,
president, Afro-American Newspapers, Baltimore, Maryland, reveals his reaction to the criticism of his book by a "topnotch Negro
critic":

> . . . he [the critic] did not review the book: he reviewed his
> prejudices against modern poetry. Let us look at some of them.
> He is against "an addendum of notes." This bias started in 1800,
> when William Wordsworth published the Preface to "Lyrical Bal-
> lads." For two hundred years poets have given prefaces or notes
> to readers. T. S. Eliot, the *only* American poet to win the Nobel
> Prize in Literature, the Master of the Super-intellectuals, added
> notes to his epic, "The Waste Land." David Jones, in that Eng-
> lish masterpiece, "The Anabasis," uses notes. Furthermore, these
> distinguished poets have had their works explained by the best
> critics in all the little magazines and countless books of criticism.
> Critics like Empson, the greatest critical reader in the British Em-
> pire, and Blackmur, the greatest critical reader in the United
> States, have not been insulted by the "addendum of notes"; these
> critics found neither a failure to communicate nor a patronizing
> gesture—to quote [the critic]—in the poets I have cited. . . .

Now if one wants to be a modern poet, one must study modern poets—and the greatest—Stevens, Rimbaud, Blok, Eliot, Pound, et al. I have done this for twenty years. Whether I have succeeded or failed you will have to ask contemporary major poets and critics. . . .[32]

Though there are several adverse criticisms of Tolson's style in the formidable ode, John Ciardi says that "one feels a force of language and of rhythm as breathtaking as anything in the range of American poetry";[33] and Tolson's publisher thought the book might garner the Pulitzer Prize.[34] Howard Fussiner, critic, seems to disagree even with his own opinion as expressed in a review in *Phylon.* In comparing *Libretto* with Tolson's earlier *Rendezvous,* he says, "a better digested, newer fashion has, combined with his natural growth, given Tolson a mature voice of considerable power," yet in the next paragraph he states, "I feel . . . that the work [*Libretto*] is not helped by its emphasis on esoteric virtuosity. . . ."[35] There is no question that critical opinion about *Libretto* is somewhat contradictory. Tolson himself felt that the whole situation surrounding his selection as poet laureate of Liberia and his writing the occasional poem were paradoxical—he was a Negro poet who was not a Negro writing about a Negro subject which was not Negro: although he was called *Negro,* he had French and Indian blood in his veins; his subject was Negro in a sense, but the Negro is only one part of the Liberian story.

Three important critics of modern American poetry praised *Libretto* with the reservation that time was needed to establish it in its true place in American literature. Tate was curious to see the influence it would have on black poetry in the United States.[36] Ciardi also recommended it as a book to return to, "for the blast of language and vision is simply too overwhelming for first judgments."[37] And twelve years after its publication, Karl Shapiro proclaimed that "The *Libretto* pulls the rug out from under the poetry of the Academy; on the stylistic level, outpounding Pound, it shocks the learned into a recognition of their own ignorance." He added, however, that, at the distance of a decade, it may be "too early for the assimilation of such a poem, even by poets."[38]

Tolson read the criticisms of *Libretto* with interest. Among his notes is this statement about the New Poetry and its critics: "A modern poem is like an iceberg—much of it is beneath the surface in shapes of ledges, bulges, crevices, warm and cold edges, colors and shadows of colors, etc. Critics are deep sea divers, exploding the poem. Some have sharper, better technique and equipment than others. They can stay submerged longer than others. For the pressure down there in a work of art may be terrific."

Years of reading, contemplation, and analysis had gone into the writing of *Libretto;* and, for a time, Tolson believed that he had written himself out. If the "horizontal audience" did not respond en masse, if the critics preferred to leave the final evaluation to time, so be it. He had satisfied his own requirements: a work of art must give intelligence a new stance, and a good poem should conjure up the ghosts of retrospection and introspection. He was content to place *Libretto* on the scales of artistic merit and to let time be the judge.

CHAPTER *4*

Harlem Gallery: Book I, The Curator

> ". . . the ambivalence of dark dark laughter rings
> in Harlem's immemorial winter."
> —Tolson, *Harlem Gallery*

*H*ARLEM GALLERY: *Book I, The Curator* is a work of art, a sociological commentary, an intellectual triple somersault. Jack Bickham, Oklahoma novelist and journalist, states that it is impossible to describe *Harlem Gallery;* and he then accepts his own challenge: "Start with the brilliance and technical virtuosity of T. S. Eliot, add the earthy power of Whitman, toss in a dash of Frost, overlay with the Negro viewpoint from Louis Armstrong to Malcolm X to Martin Luther King, and perhaps you have a hint." [1] As has been noted earlier, Tolson planned the book as the initial work of a five-volume epic poem depicting the story of the black man in America, past and present—in his words, as an introduction to "the souls of Black folk." The Curator of the Harlem Gallery, Tolson's protagonist, calls the book an "autobio-fragment"; but it is erroneous to assume that the Curator *is* Tolson. He often does speak for the author, but in some instances he does not. In "Upsilon," when the Curator and his good friend Doctor Nkomo, Bantu expatriate and Africanist, debate metaphorically about "cream" and "milk," for instance, Doctor Nkomo's arguments for "homogenized milk"—a mixture of the races and a raising of the masses—is more synonymous with Tolson's stance expressed in conversation, lectures, newspaper articles, and poetry than the Curator's preference for "cream"—the elite—or his advice to both "*taste* the milk of the skimmed/and *sip* the cream of the skimmers" (125) during this "people's dusk of dawn" (19). In fact, the Curator admits later to a "failure of nerve," which makes Doctor Nkomo the better man (133).

Though it took Tolson over a decade to produce *Harlem Gal-*

lery and though he spent long hours revising, searching for a better word or descriptive phrase or metaphor, he enjoyed writing the book. It focuses on the two subjects which interested him most: the Afro-American and art; and he gives particular attention to the plight of the twentieth-century black artist. Not only does he elaborate philosophically on his favorite subjects, but he delights in making use of his experience as a dramatist and long-time student of man to create several memorable characters, a few of which are Mr. Guy Delaporte III, "black bourgeois" president of Bola Boa Enterprises, and his wife, whom he is unable to "lead captive"; Black Orchid, Delaporte's blues-singing, striptease mistress; John Laugart, half-blind Harlem artist and murder victim; and Black Diamond, heir-presumptive of the Lenox policy racket in the ghetto. The Curator, a black intellectual ex-professor of art, introduces the reader to the highbrows, middlebrows, and lowbrows wandering through the Harlem Gallery. Playing a "minor vocative part" in the drama art, the Curator is the axis around which the subjects of black Americans, art, and the black artist revolve. Tolson characterizes his title character in this way:

> The Curator is of Afroirishjewish ancestry. He is an octoroon, who is a Negro in New York and a white man in Mississippi. Like Walter White, the late executive of the N.A.A.C.P., and the author of *A Man Called White*, the Curator is a "voluntary" Negro. Hundreds of thousands of octoroons like him have vanished into the Caucasian race—never to return. This is a great joke among Negroes. So Negroes ask the rhetorical question, "What white man is white?" We never know the real name of the Curator. The Curator is both physiologically and psychologically "The Invisible Man." He, as well as his darker brothers, think in Negro. Book One is his autobiography. He is a cosmopolite, a humanist, a connoisseur of the fine arts, with catholicity of taste and interest. He knows intimately lowbrows and middlebrows and highbrows.[2]

The characters of *Harlem Gallery* are mostly imaginary, but many of them have their origin in people Tolson had known. The prototype of Doctor Nkomo was one of Tolson's colleagues when he taught in Marshall, Texas: "As an agnostic alien professor, he almost wrecked Wiley College, proudly Methodist. . . . Nkomo, African and Africanist, is buried in the Black Belt of East Texas.

. . ." [3] Of more importance from a literary standpoint than the identity of the characters are their originality and Tolson's depth of characterization, as well as the variety of subjects which the Curator and his friends and acquaintances discuss. The conversations range from philosophy to Peeping Toms; the method of presentation alternates from dramatization to discursiveness; the form varies from poetry in the modern vein to folk ballads.

Many critics have called attention to the success of Tolson's characterization in *Harlem Gallery*. Virginia Scott Miner predicts that the characters will likely "become part of the language." [4] A reviewer for Australia's *Poetry* magazine considers the best quality of the work to be the "humour with which these strange but simple people make their entrances and exits as incidents in Tolson's mind." [5] Laurence Lieberman says the characters are "literary oddities" which "sparkle like ornaments in the vast mosaic of the book." [6] Tolson was particularly pleased by the comment of Robert Donald Spector in *Saturday Review* that "there is a 'somethingness' that stirs in all his characters: desires, ambitions, frustrations, and failures" which serve once more as a response to "Gertrude Stein's charge that the Negro 'suffers from Nathingness.' " [7]

I   *Genesis of* Harlem Gallery: Book I, The Curator

The book *Harlem Gallery* evolved from the series of character sketches entitled "A Gallery of Harlem Portraits," which Tolson composed in the 1930's. In an interview in 1965, he described the conception of his last book:

Tolson: In 1930 I was a student, on a Rockefeller Fellowship, at Columbia University. I met there a dreamer from the University of Iowa, who was trying to put together a Proustian novel. . . . One day I showed my young white friend a sonnet that I had written. It was titled "Harlem." He read it two or three times, and then said fretfully, "Melvin, Harlem is too big for a sonnet." That was the genesis of the *Harlem Gallery*.

Interviewer: But that was in 1930—thirty-five years ago.

Tolson: I know it seems like an age. The first finished manuscript of the *Harlem Gallery* was written in free verse. That was the fashion introduced by the Imagists. It contained 340 pages. *The*

Spoon River Anthology of Edgar Lee Masters was my model.
Browning's psychology in characterization stimulated me. I had
deserted the great Romantics and Victorians. Walt Whitman's ex-
uberance was in the marrow of my bones. I peddled the manuscript in the New York market. Nobody wanted it. The publishers
and critics said for commercial reasons. A few of the poems appeared in V. F. Calverton's *Modern Quarterly*. Then I stashed the
manuscript in my trunk for twenty years. At the end of that time
I had read and absorbed the techniques of Eliot, Pound, Yeats,
Baudelaire, Pasternak and, I believe, all the great Moderns. God
only knows how many "little magazines" I studied, and how much
textual analysis [*sic*] of the New Critics. To make a long story
short, the new *Harlem Gallery* was completed, and now it is
published.[8]

As a result of these years of study, Tolson evolved an intricate,
modernistic style which has caught the attention of all of the
critics who have written about *Harlem Gallery*.

II   *Form and Content of* Harlem Gallery

The style which marks both *Libretto* and *Harlem Gallery* is
based, first, on what Tolson referred to, perhaps a bit redundantly
but in keeping with his style of emphasis, as his "3-S Trinity" and,
second, on his knowledge of grammar, which determines the line
length and the stanzaic formation. Climax is the ladder of interest
by which the reader moves through the long ode, which is com-
prised of twenty-four divisions named for the Greek alphabet.
One critic points out Tolson's technical virtuosity in keeping the
eye moving down the page by centering long and short lines on a
vertical axis, thereby giving the poem "a forward-thrust of great
energy and momentum" and commanding the reader to keep
reading to the end.[9]

When Tolson began *Harlem Gallery*, he had a general plan in
mind; but only as he worked did the characters and episodes begin to emerge and organize themselves. He never feared the
lengthy, formidable task he had laid out for himself; for he felt he
was well prepared. He was steeped in tradition and in modern
literary tendencies; and he had been for years a teacher of men, a
student of man. Such an environment would surely prove dry
tinder for the spark of artistic imagination smoldering inside. He

has the Curator say of himself: "within the flame is a core/of gas
as yet unburnt/and undetected like an uninflected spoor" (25).

The plaudits of Karl Shapiro's prepublication review, published
later as the Introduction to *Harlem Gallery*, turned the attention
of much of the literary world to Tolson's work. Describing the
book as "a narrative work so fantastically stylized that the mind
balks at comparisons," Shapiro wrote of the content:

> The milieu is Harlem from the Twenties on. The dramatis per-
> sonae comprise every symbolic character, from the black bour-
> geois babbitt and the Lenox Avenue poet to the alienated Negro
> Professor and sage who sits in the bar and elaborates, along with
> the Curator and others, a Platonic dialogue. The give-and-take
> ostensibly moves on a level of talk about the arts—a "floor" which
> is constantly caving in and plunging the reader into the depth of
> metaphysical horror which journalists nowadays refer to as the
> Race Question.[10]

III   *"Alpha," "Beta," "Gamma," "Delta," "Epsilon"*

The five initial sections of *Harlem Gallery* introduce the themes
to be pursued throughout the poem: the situation of the Afro-
American and the role of the artist, particularly the black artist.
They also clarify the relationship of the Curator to the Harlem
Gallery, his work, his age, his people, and himself as he muses
about man, art, the artist, and about his own role as a black artist
in twentieth-century America. *Harlem Gallery* opens with a series
of metaphors which set the tone of the poem and establish Tolson
as a satirist of the first order:

> The Harlem Gallery, an Afric pepper bird,
>   awakes me at a people's dusk of dawn.
> The age altars its image, a dog's hind leg,
>   and hazards the moment of truth in pawn.
> . . . .
> Although the gaffing *"Tò tí?"* of the Gadfly girds
>   the I-ness of my humanness and Negroness,
>   the clockbird's
>   jackass laughter
>   in sun, in rain,
>   at dusk of dawn,

mixes with the pepper bird's reveille in my brain,
where the plain is twilled and the twilled is plain.
(19,20)

Tolson explained the three phrases which "bear a weighty
theme as metaphors": the Afric pepper bird is the alarm clock on
the West Coast of Africa, the continent from which some of the
Curator's ancestors came; "A people's dusk of dawn" is an allusion
to the title of a book, *Dusk of Dawn*, by W. E. B. DuBois, a
founder of the National Association for the Advancement of
Colored People and of the Pan-African Congress in Paris, a person
whom Tolson admired greatly; and, for the black man, the sun
will also rise—in time. The Curator, a man of fine sensibility,
hears the "jackass laughter" of the Australian clockbird, which,
unlike the pepper bird, laughs at both dusk and dawn: "The metaphor and symbol represents the scorn of Negrophobes." [11]

The age, though still tainted with racial injustice, congratulates
itself on its liberal attitude; but, to the Curator, it is "a dog's hind
leg." The poet changes the noun *altar* to a verb, making a pun of
the alliterative word. He supports his characterization of the age
in the first stanza with juxtaposed allusions from literature, art,
and history. Laden with connotation, these allusions summon up
gory, strife-torn scenes of revolution:

> The Lord of the House of Flies,
> jaundice-eyed, synapses purled,
> wries before the tumultuous canvas,
> *The Second of May*—
> by Goya:
> the dagger of Madrid
> vs.
> the scimitar of Murat.
> (19)

These lines illustrate the influence of sight, sound, and sense.
The poet's knowledge of grammar and sentence structure determines the length of the line. The first line contains the subject of
the sentence, which is suggestive of the devil or Beelzebub;[12] and
it also carries with it the nightmarish connotation of William
Golding's novel *Lord of the Flies* (1954). Parallel compound adjectives constitute line two, and line three contains the predicate.

Line four names Goya's painting and is an appositive to the last word in the preceding line. Line five, a brief prepositional phrase, identifies the painter. Lines six and eight are parallel in construction: nouns are preceded by *the* and followed by the preposition *of,* and the proper nouns serve as objects. Line seven is the single *vs.,* which separates and balances lines six and eight. Throughout the poem the lines divide consistently according to a grammatical logic that assists in interpretation.

"Alpha" concludes with additional commentary on the "Great White World," which labors, yet cannot deliver, the decision that will hasten the dawn.

> In Africa, in Asia, on the Day
> of Barricades, alarm birds bedevil the Great White World,
> a Buridan's ass—not Balaam's—between no oats and hay.
> (19)

The Curator pictures himself as an occasionally absurd, often-abused figure. As he travels through "man's Saharic up-and-down," sometimes a "Roscius as tragedian," sometimes a "Kean as clown," he occasionally musters a "rich Indies cargo." More often, however, he hears

> . . . a dry husk-of-locust blues
> descend the tone ladder of a laughing goose,
> syncopating between
> the faggot and the noose:
> "Black Boy, O Black Boy,
> is the port worth the cruise?"
> (20)

Though the Curator's spirit sometimes "wears away" in the "dust-bowl of abuse," the sense of values and inner strength which shield him against the clockbird's "jackass laughter" surface often in the sections which follow.

"Beta" opens with the Curator's philosophical speculation

> O Tempora
> *what* is man?
> (Pull down the ladder of sophistry!)
> O Mores,

what *manner* of man is this?
(Guy the ologists in effigy!)
(21)

The Curator answers his question by saying that no one knows
"the archimedean pit and pith of a man." Even to explore it,

one needs the clarity
the comma gives the eye,
not the head of the hawk
swollen with rye.
(21)

These lines demonstrate the poet's method of interspersing lines
of meter with rhythmical but unmetrical lines. Always, sight,
sound, sense, and grammatical logic dictate the length of line. The
parallelism of the first three lines and the second three lines in the
"O Tempora" passage establishes the relationship of the questions
and introduces the discussion which leads to the Curator's self-
analysis. In the four-line excerpt, the alliterative *c*'s and *h*'s and
the predominantly iambic trimeter lines with *abcb* rhyme scheme
make for unity and smoothness of expression. These lines are
among the many quotable lines which appear in the poem. Such
phrases as "the clarity the comma gives the eye" and "the head of
the hawk/swollen with rye" appeal to the senses.

The Curator's thoughts then drift from generalizations about
man to the "minor vocative part" he has played in art. Though he
speaks knowledgeably of the agony of the artist in later sections,
his tone is light:

"Great minds require of us a reading glass;
great souls, a hearing aid."
But I
in the shuttlebox world,
again and again,
have both mislaid.
(22)

The Curator is an ex-professor of art, his identity "gored" by rou-
tine. Like his creator, he feels that the upper rungs of his ladder

are "zeroes." Each has observed with interest the angry young
artists of succeeding generations—The Lost, The Bright, The
Angry, The Beat. They, too, have worked to reshape the thoughts
and dreams of each decade, refusing to "stoop the neck to die/like
a dunghill cock" (25).

"Gamma" equates art with a "babel city in the people's Shinar"
where "sweating pilgrims" jostle about and apostates dodge
apostles' arrows. The Curator takes hope, however, as he recalls
his "Afroirishjewish" grandfather's faith in man's ability to sur-
vive, though " 'Between the dead sea Hitherto/and the promised
land Hence/looms the wilderness Now . . .' " (27). These lines
illustrate the epigrammatic quality which appears frequently in
the poem. Often the metaphor teams with parallelism, and sometimes personification, producing succinct lines of wit.

"Delta" advances the choice of the artist: God or Caesar. There
is no point in probing the artist's motive, the Curator says,
whether the work is "for Ars',/the Cathedra's, or the Agora's sake"
(29); for only the result is important. The artist must have courage, for he endures his pain alone—a "St. John's agony . . . without a St. John's fire—" (31). Though one man is willed "the wings
of an eagle" and another "the teats of a sow," no man should sneer
at his fellow man. Neither should he envy him: "Let thy blue eyes
resist white stars of red desire" (32). Equally colorful is the simile
which pictures art as being "unique as the white tiger's/pink paws
and blue eyes . . ." (33).

Whereas "Delta" considers the definition of art and the "true"
artist, "Epsilon" moves to a consideration of the various pressures
brought to bear upon the artist by "the idols of the tribe," who
demand that he celebrate *their* heroes. The Curator recalls that
"Milton's Lucifer was a Cavalier—/his God, a Roundhead" (34).
The artist's heroes are not necessarily those of the "bulls of
Bashan," who exert power, serving

> . . . Belshazzarian tables to artists and poets who
>   serve the hour,
>   torn between two masters,
>   God and Caesar—
>   this (for Conscience),
>   the Chomolungma of disasters.
>
>   (36)

To understand the full implications of the Curator's references to "the Idols of the Tribe" and the "bulls of Bashan" requires a knowledge not only of English literature and the Bible but of the sociological work *Black Bourgeoisie* (1957) written by a Howard University professor whom Tolson admired, E. Franklin Frazier. "Black Bourgeoisie" is the term Frazier uses to describe those members of the black middle class who have separated themselves from their folk background and have "accepted unconditionally the values of the white bourgeois world: its morals and its canons of respectability, its standards of beauty and consumption." [13] Frazier says that, because the white world has continued to reject the black bourgeoisie, the blacks have developed a deepseated inferiority complex. To compensate, they have created a world of make-believe to "escape the disdain of whites and fulfill their wish for status in American life." [14] The tendency to glamorize social life makes "socialites" of the Negroes considered newsworthy: "The exaggerated importance which the black bourgeoisie attaches to 'society' is revealed in the emphasis placed by the Negro press upon the social aspects of events concerning Negroes." [15]

Thus, "Epsilon" opens with "the Idols of the Tribe" bellowing, "We/have heroes! Celebrate them upon our walls!" (34). Tolson regarded such "Cadillac Philistines" (57) with amusement and pity. Truth, he believed, demanded that he celebrate the lowbrows of Afro-America as well as the middlebrows and the highbrows; and he knew that the black bourgeoisie would be wondering, "What will the white folks think?" Indeed, Tolson's decision not to give the Curator a name, according to his notes on *Harlem Gallery*, was done with the ironic awareness that among the black bourgeoisie, such a title would be deserving of great respect:

> Degrees and titles have fabulous status value. Nobody wants to be a nobody; everybody wants to be Somebody! So a title makes the *possessor* and the *Race* Somebody in the Great White World. Professor, Doctor, the Honorable, Reverend, Grand Basileus, President, Grand Polemarch, Judge, etc. So white folk can't call these "Boy" and "Uncle." Degrees and titles in the Negro world have individual and ethnic survival value. When a Negro achieves in the Arts or Sports, his Great I Am runs through the Race like electricity along a wire. If he messes up, the same thing occurs. So Negroes who never go to the Harlem Gallery get a kick

out of the title *The Curator*. It's a new title and shows that the
Race is going places.[16]

The Curator, along with his intellectual friends John Laugart, artist, and Doctor Nkomo, elaborates on the black bourgeoisie in
later sections. Tolson was aware that the intrusion of the Frazier
terminology and philosophy into the poem would not make for
popularity among those readers who disagree with the theses
Frazier propounds in *Black Bourgeoisie*. Some of Frazier's asser-
tions about a segment of the black population in the United States
would be considered not as explanatory but as derogatory. Tolson
anticipated this reaction. Sensitive to the black artist's problem of
satisfying both a black and white audience, Tolson stated that, if
the white artist is *alienated* in this country, the black artist is *anni-
hilated*. He desired recognition—even popularity—from his own
race; but he would not compromise with what he believed to be
the truth about either black or white Americans.

IV "Zeta," "Eta," "Theta," "Iota"

In the first five sections of *Harlem Gallery* the reader overhears
the Curator's soliloquies on the central themes of the book. In the
next two sections, "Zeta" and "Eta," the reader meets two of the
Curator's friends, John Laugart and Doctor Nkomo; the third section, "Theta," is a short philosophical commentary which blends
together the seemingly disparate subjects of art, the gap between
the races, and happiness; in the fourth, "Iota," the Curator and
Doctor Nkomo contemplate on black Americans as they greet the
patrons of the Harlem Gallery. These four sections, "Zeta," "Eta,"
"Theta," and "Iota," contain the two major types of presentation
in *Harlem Gallery*—discursiveness and dramatization. Thirteen of
the twenty-four sections of the book are largely discursive, while
the remaining eleven are primarily dramatic. Several sections,
such as "Iota," combine the two methods.

"Zeta" dramatizes some of the temptations and pressures the
artist suffers which are defined in "Epsilon." The Curator visits the
catacomb Harlem flat of his half-blind painter friend John Laugart, who, though he starves, will "never sell/mohair for alpaca/to
ring the bell!" (41). He sees Laugart's painting, *Black Bourgeoisie*
(Tolson's notes indicate that the painting was inspired by Fra-

zier's book *Black Bourgeoisie*), and thinks to himself that it will
evoke a "Jeremian cry" from the "babbitted souls" of the eyeless
regents of Harlem Gallery. Laugart, who reads the Curator's
thoughts, assures him that he is not concerned about the fate of
his work of art, regardless of the disapproval of the regents or
anyone else:

> A work of art
> is an everlasting flower
> in kind or unkind hands;
> dried out,
> it does not lose its form and color
> in native or in alien lands.
>
> (39)

Laugart's courage, as expressed in his philosophy and in his life,
makes him one of the memorable characters in *Harlem Gallery;*
he appears but briefly, then is robbed and murdered in his flat,
with only a "hamletian rat" for witness. His sense of values is un-
derscored clearly as he tells the Curator,

> It matters not a tinker's dam
> on the hither or thither side of the Acheron
> how many rivers you cross
> if you fail to cross the Rubicon!
>
> (42)

Though John Laugart's work brought him only "a bottle of
Schiedam gin/and Charon's grin/and infamy" (42), his courage,
the Curator implies, is the stuff of which true art is made.

In "Eta" the Curator goes to Aunt Grindle's Elite Chitterling
Shop, where he encounters Doctor Obi Nkomo, "the alter ego/of
the Harlem Gallery," who reaffirms Picasso's statement, "The lie
of the artist is the only lie/for which a mortal or a god should die"
(43). To the African, "Nobody was a nobody"; and, though irony
occasionally escapes his lips, no malice is intended. He "calls the
hand" of his Americanized brethren because of the dichotomy he
sees between their theory and practice of democracy and Christianity.

When a dope-sniffing "giraffine fellow" asks curiously, "Mister,

who are you?," Doctor Nkomo replies with a Zulu story which
scarcely enlightens the "Ixion bound/to the everlasting revolving
ghetto wheel" (50). A hunter once found an eagle in a chicken
yard; he took it to a mountaintop and threw it into space; it tum-
bled down, "a ghostified cock," when suddenly another eagle
swooped out of the sky, "clarioning the summons of an aeried
race." The barnyard eagle answered twice, then

thrice
he spiraled the simoom-blistered height—
braked and banked and beaked
upward, upward, into transfiguring light.
Old Probabilities, *what* am I?
Mister, *what* are you?
An eagle or a chicken come home to roost?
I wish I knew!

(51)

Here, as throughout the poem, the grammatical structure determines the line length. A natural pause comes at the end of each
line, even when punctuation is not used. The word *thrice* is emphasized because it stands alone. Line two contains the independ-
ent clause in the sentence. The next line consists of three parallel,
alliterative verbs connected with the coordinate conjunction *and*
followed by a slight pause which gives impetus to the words *upward* at the beginning of line four. Each of the last four lines is a
sentence, a logical break occurring at the end of each line. The
sound of the alliterative and onomatopoeic *spiraled, simoom* and
blistered, banked, braked, beaked exhibit the artistry of the poet
who is guided by his "3-S" formula. The contrast between the
eagle which "thrice . . . spiraled the simoom-blistered height"
and the commonplace wording of the final question—are you "an
eagle or a chicken come home to roost?"—intensifies the comic
effect. It parallels the intellectual level of the "yellow giraffine fellow" who asks the philosophical Africanist, "Mister, *who* are you?"
and the esoteric Doctor Nkomo whose answer is lost on him.

When Doctor Nkomo loses his temper momentarily with Mr.
Guy Delaporte III, shogun of Bola Boa Enterprises, Inc., and the
prime example of Frazier's black bourgeoisie, the Africanist apol-
ogizes with sincerity:

I've called the gentleman a liar
—it's true—
and I am sorry for it.
(52)

The wit of Doctor Nkomo, in calling Delaporte a liar a second
time in his "apology" and the poet's mastery of the three S's with
emphasis on alliteration, onomatopoeia, parallelism, and imagery
make for effectiveness both in content and style.

The brief "Theta" section emphasizes the unifying power of art.
The poet juxtaposes phrases from Frost and Blake in this
passage:

Something there is in Art that does not love a wall.
Idea and image,
form and content,
blend like pigment with pigment
in a flesh color.
What dread hand can unmix
pink and yellow?
(54)

Art, the Curator says, unites Montague's son and Capulet's daughter as "the miracle of the metaphor smites/disparate realms into a
form/tighter than a mailed fist" (55). Both art and nature explore
the whole as they "ignore/the outer and the inner/of a person/a
place, a thing . . ." (55).

"Iota" changes the emphasis from art to various types of Afro-
Americans as the Curator and Doctor Nkomo welcome the "gob-
bler-breasted matrons" and their spouses to the Harlem Gallery.
As the Curator looks through the four wings of the gallery, he sees
portraits of Negroid diversity—of "Kafiristan gaucherie" and "At-
tic wit and nerve." The gallery is "Harlem's Aganippe/(not America's itching aitchbone)!" (60).

The "Idols of the Tribe" once more demand that *their* heroes be
celebrated. Doctor Nkomo chuckles, for his hobby is tracing family lines. What has he discovered about even the "best" of fami-
lies?

If
a Bourbon should shake his family tree

long enough . . . he
—beyond a Diogenic doubt—
would kneel at the mourners' bench,
dressed in black crepe,
as cannibal and idiot,
rapist and ape,
tumble out.

(62)

Just as the Bourbons are made up of cannibals and kings, so the Curator sees among the visitors to the gallery both "gentlemen and galoots."

V   "Kappa," "Lambda," "Mu," "Nu," "Xi"

In "Kappa," "Lambda," "Mu," "Nu," and "Xi" the reader meets an array of intriguing characters who meander through the Harlem Gallery. He sees them through the eyes of the Curator and Doctor Nkomo, who consider them psychologically and philosophically as they analyze them dispassionately but with understanding and a sense of humor. Mr. and Mrs. Guy Delaporte III, who make an appearance in "Kappa," "oh and yawn and ah" their way through Harlem's Vanity Fair,

he,
with a frown like curd;
she,
with a smile like whey.
(64)

The successful president of Bola Boa Enterprises, Inc., is the symbol of Churchianity at Mount Zion, where the Sugar Hill elite worship. He is unhappy because no "brand-new $-world in Harlem gives him pause" and because he cannot master his wife, with her "incurves and outcurves of breasts and hips." Bishop Euphorbus Harmsworth attempts to shield her from her husband's anger. When Mr. Delaporte spies Laugart's painting *Black Bourgeoisie*, he is "a wounded Cape buffalo defying everything and Everyman!" (65). When, nearby, the Curator and Doctor Nkomo observe his reaction, Nkomo remarks approvingly that the "mirage of the Status Quo," undisturbed, "chokes the vitals." The Curator agrees that it is time to *"give voice to a bill/of faith at another hour"* (67). Despite pressure and atrocities, the *élan* of the artist survives.

The next four sections—"Lambda," "Mu," "Nu," and "Xi"—belong to the "vagabond bard of Lenox Avenue," Hideho Heights, one of the most colorful characters who frequents the Harlem Gallery. He announces his arrival with a voice like "a ferry horn in a river of fog": "Hey, man, when you gonna close this dump?/Fetch highbrow stuff for the middlebrows who/don't give a damn and the lowbrows who ain't hip!" (68). His excuse for being late exemplifies the wit characteristic of much of the dialogue: "Sorry, Curator, I got here late:/my black ma birthed me in the Whites' bottom drawer,/and the Reds forgot to fish me out!" (68). Fresh from a jam session at the Daddy-O Club Hideho folds his lips about the neck of a bottle of "white-heat hooch" and begins to chant his most recent inspiration—a tribute to Louis Armstrong:

> *King Oliver of New Orleans*
> *has kicked the bucket, but he left behind*
> *old Satchmo with his red-hot horn*
> *to syncopate the heart and mind.*
> *The honky-tonks in Storyville*
> *have turned to ashes, have turned to dust,*
> *but old Satchmo is still around*
> like Uncle Sam's *IN GOD WE TRUST.*
>
> *Where, oh, where is Bessie Smith*
> *with her heart as big as the blues of truth?*
> *Where, oh, where is Mister Jelly Roll*
> *with his Cadillac and diamond tooth?*
> *Where, oh, where is Papa Handy*
> *with his blue notes a-dragging from bar to bar?*
> *Where, oh, where is bulletproof Leadbelly*
> *with his tall tales and 12-string guitar?*
>
> *Old Hip Cats,*
> *when you sang and played the blues*
> *the night Satchmo was born,*
> *did you know hypodermic needles in Rome*
> *couldn't hoodoo him away from his horn?*
> *Wyatt Earp's legend, John Henry's, too,*

*is a dare and a bet to old Satchmo
when his groovy blues put headlines in the news
from the Gold Coast to cold Moscow.*

*Old Satchmo's
gravelly voice and tapping foot and crazy notes
set my soul on fire.
If I climbed
the seventy-seven steps of the Seventh
Heaven, Satchmo's high C would carry me higher!
Are you hip to this, Harlem? Are you hip?
On Judgment Day, Gabriel will say
after he blows his horn:
"I'd be the greatest trumpeter in the Universe,
if old Satchmo had never been born!"*
(69–70)

The ballad builds from a relatively regular iambic tetrameter
line in the first two eight-line sections to a freer metrical and
rhyme pattern in the last two sections. Why does the poet vary the
rhythm and rhyme scheme as the poem moves along? The "song"
builds to a climax in the fourth part, and the "singer" requires
freedom to express the emotion which cannot be restrained by a
regular pattern. The ballad which begins with the statement that
"old Satchmo is still around"—expressed in comparatively regular meter and rhyme scheme, reaches an intensity in *"Old
Satchmo's/gravelly voice and tapping foot and crazy notes/set my
soul on fire"* (70). The emotion builds with Hideho's theoretical
climb up the *"seventy-seven steps of the Seventh/Heaven"*—the
poet depending heavily on alliteration here rather than on metrical pattern—where *"Satchmo's high C would carry me higher."*
The seriocomic treatment of Satchmo begins with King Oliver
"kicking the bucket." It climaxes with the Judgment Day image of
Gabriel, who blows his horn and then admits, *"I'd be the greatest
trumpeter in the Universe/if old Satchmo had never been
born!"*
Hideho's dramatic presentation of his tribute to "Old Satchmo"
has set the mood; and in "Mu," the Zulu Club "black cats, are
gone!" (74). A vixen wearing a tight Park Avenue skirt does the
Lenox Avenue Quake. The Curator says, "Jazz is the philosophers'
egg of the Whites" (74). Hideho juxtaposes a Shakespearian

image into the caricature of his host as he satirizes the Great
White World:

> Yonder Curator has a lean and hungry look;
> he thinks too much.
> Such blackamoors are dangerous to
> the Great White World!
>
> (76)

In "Nu" the M. C., Rufino Laughlin, introduces Hideho as the
guest poet for the evening. A "tipsy Lena" peddling "Edenic
joys" proposes,

> If you make me a poem,
> Hideho,
> I'll make you my one and only daddy-o
> till the Statue of Liberty
> dates
> a kinkyhead.
>
> (78)

Hideho does not respond to her proposal, but he presents in "Xi"
to his delighted audience his epic entitled "John Henry," the hero
of which Tolson referred to as the Beowulf of the Afro-American.
As the crowd awaits his performance, "Sudden silence,/succulent
as the leaves of a fat hen, swallowed/up the Zulu Club" (79). The
image of the yellow folds of internal fat which flavor the hen,
combined with the alliterative words *sudden, silence, succulent,*
and *swallowed* appeal to the senses of taste and hearing. These
and the attention to line division—the pause after *silence* and the
balanced words *swallowed* and *succulent* which begin and end
the second line—demonstrate the "3-S" formula. The allure of colorful words is also evident in these lines describing Hideho's
stance:

> He staged a brown pose that minded me
> of an atheistic black baritone
> who sang blue spirituals that turned
> some white folk white, some pink, and others red.
>
> (79)

Such lines seem to satisfy the poet's compulsion to play with words and images as well as exhibit his sense of humor.

Hideho begins his account of "John Henry," a folk ballad in the tradition of American humor and tall tales with a sharp, stinging wit. Hideho is in his element here as the "people's poet"; he and his audience interact as he chants the opening lines in a "faraway funereal voice." His audience interrupts and accompanies him in response to his poetic tribute to the superhuman characteristics and exploits of the heroic John Henry:

> The night John Henry was born
> no Wise Men came to his cabin because
> they got lost in a raging storm
> that tore
> the countryside apart
> like a mother's womb
> when a too-big son is born.
>   (80)

Dipsy Muse cries, "Great God A' Mighty" and squeezes his fat spouse. Murmurs ebb and flow. Hideho continues,

> *The night John Henry is born an ax*
> *of lightning splits the sky*
> *and a hammer of thunder pounds the earth,*
> *and the eagles and panthers cry!*
>   (81)

Wafer Waite, an ex-peon who has survived a Texas tornado, cries, "Didn't John Henry's Ma and Pa/get no warning?" Hideho replies, "Brother,/the tornado alarm became/tongue-tied."

> *John Henry—he says to his Ma and Pa:*
> *"Get a gallon of barley corn.*
> *I want to start right, like a he-man child,*
> *the night that I am born!"*
>   (81)

The audience whoops and stomps, "clap thighs, backs and knees."

"Says: "I want some ham hocks, ribs, and jowls
a pot of cabbage and greens;
some hoecakes, jam, and buttermilk;
a platter of pork and beans!"

John Henry's Ma—she wrings her hands,
and his Pa—he scratches his head.
John Henry—he curses in giraffe-tall words,
flops over, and kicks down the bed.

He's burning mad, like a bear on fire—
so he tears to the riverside.
As he stoops to drink, Old Man River gets scared
and runs upstream to hide!

Some say he was born in Georgia—O Lord!
Some say in Alabam.
But it's writ on the rock at the Big Bend Tunnel:
"Lousyana was my home. So scram!"
                    . . . .
I was born in Bitchville, Lousyana.
A son of Ham, I had to scram!
I was born in Bitchville, Lousyana:
so I ain't worth a T.B. damn!
                    . . . .
Ma taught me to pray. Pa taught me to grin,
It pays, Black Boy; oh, it pays!
So I pray to God and grin at the Whites
in seventy-seven different ways!

I came to Lenox Avenue.
Poor Boy Blue! Poor Boy Blue!
I came to Lenox Avenue,
but I find up here a Bitchville, too! [17]
                                         (82–84)

Hideho drinks in the applause of the Zulu Club Wits, along
with a swig that would "make/a squirrel spit in the eye of a bull-
dog" (82). Next, an ex-professor of philosophy, Joshua Nitze, en-
tertains the Wits with an anecdote on integration, in which a
black stevedore went into an elite restaurant in the South and was
asked by the white waitress, "What can I do for you, Mister?"
Nitze pauses to ask if they could imagine "a black man mistered

by a white dame/in the Bible Belt of the pale phallus and chalk
clitoris." When the dockhand orders chitterlings and the waitress
says they are not on the menu, he sneers, "Night and day, Ma'am,/
I've been telling Black Folks/*you* White Folks ain't ready for integration!" (85).

The laughter dies away and as the Curator and his sports editor
friend, Vincent Aveline, have a few drinks together. Aveline tells
him that a stool pigeon for Black Diamond has just informed him
that Aveline's wife is having an affair with Mr. Guy Delaporte III.
The Curator's thoughts are interrupted by his good friend Black
Diamond, a major figure in the Lenox Policy Rackets and an ex-
student of the Curator, who tells him that, if the regents of the
gallery ever think of firing the Curator, he will give the dossier he
has on each of them to Walter Winchell. He would do it anyway
were it not for race pride: "White Folks are always ready to disin-
fect the privy/of decent Black Folks . . ." (88). Besides, doing so
would set a bad example for the little guys. Black Diamond makes
sure, by paying his church dues a year in advance, that at his
funeral the preacher will not "blab" and that St. Peter will not
"gab."

Lionel Matheus then picks up the symbol of the white man as
serpent, which Shadrach Martial Kilroy, president of Afroamerican Freedom, *Incorporated,* has introduced. Matheus says that
the Afro-American is the frog which becomes, the harder it pulls
away, more impaled on the fangs of the snake. Doctor Nkomo
reminds them that the big python swallows both the little python
and the frog when the little python will not let go of the frog.
Kilroy tell Matheus that, in order for his symbols to be successful,
he needs to see

the unerring beak,
the unnerving eye,
the untiring wing,
of Afroamerican Freedom, *Incorporated*—
the Republic's secretary bird.

(91)

When Matheus says to Kilroy, "Almost thou persuadest me to be a
nigger lover," Kilroy sighs, "It is hard for a phobic camel to
go/through the eye of a needle of truth" (91). The Curator thinks

how often metaphors and symbols have been the "Negro's manna in the Great White World." The liquor and the long evening close in on Hideho, who slumps, slobbers, and sobs, "My *people,/my* people—/they know not what they do" (92).

VI   *"Omicron," "Pi"*

The "Omicron" and "Pi" sections revert to the discursive reflections of the Curator and Doctor Nkomo about art. "Omicron" contains many allusions to historical figures, biblical passages, and literature; and it stresses again the pressures on the artist. The nine concluding parts of this section elaborate on what constitutes the artist's net loss, his net profit, his pride, his *élan,* his school, his grind, his temperament, his sensibility, and his esthetic distance. In "Pi," when the Curator thinks about art, the artist, and the critics, he emphasizes the courage and integrity which are essential to the artist, despite external pressures to compromise. "Omicron" presents metaphors that define the artist and his struggle for survival:

> The school of the artist
> *is*
> the circle of wild horses,
> heads centered,
> as they present to the wolves
> a battery of heels. . . .
>   (96)

At times, the poet seems to be more intrigued with figures of speech and alliterative devices than with clarification. Such a metaphor describes the labor of the artist:

> The grind of the artist
> *is*
> the grind of the gravel in the gizzard
> of the golden eagle.
>   (97)

In other sections the "S-Trinity" works well to produce effective images:

> The esthetic distance of the artist
> *is*
> the purple foxglove
> that excites
> the thermo receptors of the heart
> and the light receptors of the brain.
> (97)

"Pi" reemphasizes the idea that, no matter how strong the external pressure becomes, the artist must keep his integrity. He cannot be a "fence-sitter." Nkomo notes that critics allow artists to go to "the holy of holies . . . or a whorehouse;/but never to/Harpers Ferry or Babii Yar or Highgate" (102). The Curator expresses Tolson's conception of the true artist in "Pi" when he says that he seeks the *how,* the *what,* and the *why* when he looks at a work of art and that the artist is concerned not with the present so much as with the future: "The harlot Now the master paints/aspires to hang in the gallery Hence . . . " (102).

VII   *"Rho," "Sigma," "Tau," "Upsilon"*

"Rho," "Sigma," "Tau," and "Upsilon" tell the story of Mr. Starks; his wife Hedda Starks, alias Black Orchid, who is a "striptease has-been/of the brassy pitband era" (103); and his *Harlem Vignettes,* character sketches of the Harlemites Starks knows only too well. These sketches bear some similarity to those appearing in Tolson's first *Harlem Gallery,* which contained a series of short poems about various Harlem characters and, as has been pointed out, was influenced both by Masters' *Spoon River Anthology* and Browning's "psychology in characterization." [18] In the later work, Starks's *Harlem Vignettes,* the influence of Masters, particularly, is not so apparent as in the original because of the difference in their styles. Tolson's revisions incorporate his "3-S" formula of sight, sound, and sense in determining the centered lines of irregular length which philosophize about the various Harlem figures by Starks in his *Vignettes.*

The action begins in "Rho" on New Year's Day when Black Orchid, Mister Starks's widow, calls the Curator after she has gone to a marijuana party, which resulted in her arrest, after which she spent an uneasy night, besieged with nightmares, in the local jail. She tells the Curator where he can find her deceased husband's manuscript, *Harlem Vignettes,* which she had stolen from him before his death. The Curator recalls that the departed Mister Starks (named *Mister* by his mother to prevent his being called *boy* or *uncle*) had been captivated by Black Orchid's "barbarian bump and sophisticated grind" the first time he had seen her. Her "exhumed liaison" with Mr. Guy Delaporte III broke his heart. He learned from this experience that "the descent to Avernus is easy" (105), but he also discovered a fast ascent.

"Sigma" relates that before his death Mister Starks sent his last will and testament to the owner of the funeral home, Ma'am Shears; and in it he requested that he be buried in the tails he had worn the night the Harlem Symphony Orchestra had premiered his *Black Orchid Suite,* that the ebony baton given to him by a West African witch doctor be placed in his hand, and that Black Orchid give the Curator the manuscript of his *Harlem Vignettes* which she had taken. When Ma'am Shears received his will, she dialed Starks's room to beg him to be sensible, saying, "It's not like Black Folks to commit suicide" (108). His remark "Aren't we civilized yet?" was lost on her, for she had never heard of Tomáš Garrigue Masaryk's statement in Vienna that only civilized peoples commit suicide. Starks then told Ma'am Shears to bring her assistant, Mr. Abelard Littlejohn, to meet him at "Archangel Gabriel's hangout/on Elysian Boulevard" (108).

"Sigma" ends on a cryptic note. The sergeant, who "knew his A. Conan Doyle from *aardvark* to *zythum*," found the bullet in Mister Starks's heart. The superintendent found the gun in Crazy Cain's toilet bowl. At last the Curator has the *Harlem Vignettes,* and "The black ox treads the wine press of Harlem" (110). "Tau," the shortest section in the poem, introduces the longest section, "Upsilon," which contains the *Harlem Vignettes.* The manuscript is tied up in a mamba skin on which is inscribed in purple-red ink, "In the sweat of thy face shalt thou make a work of art" (111). Years before, Mister Starks had published a volume of Imagist verse; and his reason for changing from the style of the Imagists to his "modern" style appears on the title page of the *Vignettes:* "I should have followed—perhaps—*Des Imagistes*/down the Macadam Road./But I'm no Boabdil/at the Last Sigh of the Moor" (111).

"Upsilon," one of the most interesting parts in *Harlem Gallery,* contains Mister Starks's portraits, the first of which is a self-portrait. Unlike Laugart and the Curator, Mister Starks did not attempt to cross the Rubicon; instead, he tried to "poise the see-saw between *want* and *have*" (112). His boogie record *Pot Belly Papa* sold a million copies, but the "sunrise on the summit" of his life was the premiere of the *Black Orchid Suite* by the Harlem Symphony Orchestra. The "fig leaf" of Black Orchid proved more powerful than the "Rosetta stone," however, and he rationalized, "So what the hell?/Am I not a Negro, a Harlemite, an artist—/a trinity that stinks the ermine robes/of the class-conscious seraphs?" (112). Nevertheless, though he could sacrifice his artistic integrity for love, he admired the true artists he saw around him.

Mister Starks's second portrait is that of Hideho Heights, "a man square as the *x* in Dixie" (113). Hideho's credo of art is that "The form and content in a picture or a song should blend like the vowels in a diphthong" (114). The "'black bourgeoise" regarded him as "a crab louse/in the pubic region of Afroamerico" (114), but it bothered him not at all. The subjects of the third and fourth portraits are Dr. Igor Shears, deceased, and his widow Ma'am Shears, who was introduced in "Sigma" as the owner of the Ange-lus Funeral Home. Mister Starks pictures Dr. Shears as a man with two loves: the arts and fishing. Though they were friends, Dr. Shears was always an enigma to Mister Starks. In contrast, Ma'am Shears's character "was a cliché in the *Book of Homilies;*/and *what she was* was as legible/as a Spencerian ad-dress/in the window of an envelope" (115).

The character sketch of Crazy Cain helps explain the meaning of the statement in "Sigma" that the gun which had killed Mister Starks was found hidden in Crazy Cain's toilet bowl. Mister Starks says that he had fired Crazy Cain from the symphony orchestra because of his harsh "primitive percussive" style. A descendant of an Irish field hand and a Mandingo woman raped in an Alabama cottonfield, Crazy Cain knew nothing of his people's past; but he had somehow intuited that he was the bastard son of Black Or-chid, now Mister Starks's wife, and Mr. Guy Delaporte III. Mister Starks ends the sketch with the comment that "his knowing fell short of the *Poudres de Succession*" (116). These facts make clear that there was likely little love between Crazy Cain and Mister

Starks; and though Tolson does not explain the "murder," perhaps
Mister Starks either provoked or persuaded Crazy Cain to kill him
as a kind of revenge against his wife and Delaporte.

Mister Starks devotes ten pages to the portraits of the two
major characters in *Harlem Gallery*: Doctor Nkomo and the
Curator. Mister Starks recalls how his friend Dr. Shears had
joshed Doctor Nkomo about his defense of socialism. The Africanist, who had laughed good-naturedly, had reminded his friend
that even Whitman, though "bedded in the Democratic Vista
Inn," had discovered that the materialism of the West was a "stea-
topygous Jezebel/with falsies on her buttocks" (118). Hideho
Heights captures Nkomo with an "Aristotelian" metaphor: "Obi
Nkomo is a St. John who envisions/a brush turkey that makes/a
mound of the old World's decaying vegetables/to generate heat
and hatch the eggs of the New" (118).

The Harlem Gallery, Mister Starks says, is a creek connecting
the island and the mainland, an oasis in the desert. One of the
"variegated aviary" that inhabit the gallery is the Curator, "a jacobin of horny, reversed epidermal outgrowths" (119); for the Curator equated Delaporte, the picture lover, with Ike, the painter,
and with Nikita, the art critic. Though the Harlem gossip sheet, a
black bourgeoisie publication, aimed its volley time and time
again at the Curator, he held his ground. Even Mr. Guy Delaporte
III begrudgingly observed that the Curator was a "Greenland
shark/feeding on the carcass of a whale/in spite of stabs
in the head!" (120). Doctor Nkomo described his friend the
Curator as a "dusky Francis I of France/with an everlasting cartel
of defiance" (121).

That Mister Starks had studied his fellow man closely is obvious
in his revelation of the difference between Nkomo and the Curator, whose ideas and values are quite similar. During one of their
predawn discussions, they talked about race and caste. Nkomo
believed that the lifting of the masses was the hope of mankind,
and he favored integration of the races. For him, the white man's
theory of the cream separator was a "stinking skeleton," a dead
theory in need of burial. The Curator, who liked to "dangle So-
cratic bait," suggested that perhaps "omniscience deigns to color-
breed" (124).

When the janitor, an ex-chaplain from Alabama Christian College, overheard the Curator's comment, he joined them to add that, according to the white man, African blood is so potent that only one drop makes the whitest Nordic an instant Negro. Perhaps, he suggests, there is hope for the black man in the symbolism of the "rich opacity of cream/and the poor whiteness of skim milk" (125). Mister Starks commented (in parentheses) that he hoped mortals would never become mind readers, for a "sex image of a Mary of Magdala/with kinky hair and a cream complexion" had just "hula-hulaed" across his mind. To the Curator, who then turned the cream-and-milk metaphor from race to class, the safest course during a time of change is the middle road: "*taste* the milk of the skimmed/and *sip* the cream of the skimmers" (125). This attitude, to Nkomo, was an "eclipse of faith." A mind conscious of uprightness dares to "peddle/the homogenized milk of multiculture" everywhere. This homogenized milk includes both the elite and the masses, as well as all races.

Mister Starks's psychoanalysis of Mrs. Guy Delaporte III explains why her husband, so successful in business enterprise and extramarital relationships, can neither understand nor control her uneven temperament. Mister Starks says she is the victim of an Electra complex; she is "a delicate plant exposed/to the arctic circle of the black Sodom" (127), Guy Delaporte, who causes her leaflets to close and her leafstalks to droop "in fits of relapsing fever" (127). The poet's images here are reminiscent of the "chills and fever" image in John Crowe Ransom's "Here Lies a Lady" in the ironic tone and sardonic humor resulting from the contrast.

In another portrait, John Laugart, to whom "Zeta" was devoted, is compared by Mister Starks to the blind, paralytic French caricaturist Honoré Daumier: "each a bowl from the Potter's wheel/the State buried in a potter's field . . ." (127). Laugart's life was too hard for any man, but he at last rests in peace. The final portrait in the *Vignettes* is of Big Mama, who was mentioned briefly in "Rho" as the one to whom Black Orchid had given the *Vignettes* for safekeeping after she had stolen her husband's manuscript. Big Mama's conscience was for sale. She had street sense, and many one hundred dollar bills had been planted in her "bediamonded claw." Her brag was, "I was born in Rat Alley./I live on Fox Avenue./I shall die in Buzzard Street" (128).

"Upsilon" closes with Mister Starks's reflections about his failure to be the artist he might have been. Again he comforts himself with the thought that, although self-pity is "conspicuous consumption of the soul," he knows, like "all 100-p.c. Negroes," that a white skin is the only way to success, freedom, justice, and equality. Occasionally, he envisions a *Rhapsody of Black and White;* but he usually squelches the thought with a bottle of bootleg and reminds himself to "Put the notes on the staff, Black Boy!" (132).

VIII   *"Phi," "Chi," "Psi," "Omega"*

In the four concluding books of *Harlem Gallery* the Curator reflects about the Afro-American, art, and the problems of the black artist. "Phi" recalls the enslavement and suffering of Africans brought to America and issues a warning to the white man to beware of the power of the black minority in this country. "Chi" considers the dilemma of the black artist who has to decide between writing poetry for popularity or posterity. "Psi" explains how the Curator—and he speaks in this section for Tolson himself —has faced the black artist's "American dilemma"; and he prophesies how America's racial strife will end. "Omega," a recapitulation of the Curator's theses, presents a final explanation of the objective of the Curator—and Tolson—in writing *Harlem Gallery* and his feeling about the work: to artistically characterize his people, revealing their depth and complexity in the light of their history and to project their future in a country which has never really recognized their many facets.

In "Phi" the Curator ponders the *Harlem Vignettes*. As he thinks of the cream-and-milk dialogue recorded by Mister Starks, he admits to himself that Nkomo is a better man than he. The conscience prick takes him back to the centuries-old suffering of his people in this poignant passage:

> Beneath the sun
> as he clutched the bars of a barracoon,
> beneath the moon
> of a blind and deaf-mute Sky,
> my forebears heard a Cameroon
> chief, in the language of the King James Bible, cry,
> "O Absalom, my son, my son!"
>   (135)

The line division once more depends on grammatical logic in what is perhaps the most subjectively emotional passage in the poem. The poet demonstrates his ability to effect feeling by using alliteration, assonance, rhyme, strong iambic and anapestic lines of varied length; by personification of the unseeing, unfeeling sky; and, finally, by pathos evoked by the allusion to King David's mourning the loss of his beloved son.

Tolson follows this subjective, metrical passage with unmetered lines which jerk the reader back to a safe distance from the highly emotional scene he has just witnessed. The "blind and deaf-mute sky" image is reminiscent of the "purblind Doomsters" who people Thomas Hardy's poems and novels, where life is inevitably tragic. To secure objectivity and distance, the poet then has Hideho Heights treat the Zulu Club Wits to his most recent inspiration: the story of an encounter between a sea turtle and a shark. The symbolic story relates how the shark swallows the turtle whole. Then, when the turtle's descent is completed,

> with ravenous jaws
> that can cut sheet steel scrap,
> the sea-turtle gnaws
> . . . and gnaws . . . and gnaws . . .
> his way in a way that appalls—
> *his* way to freedom,
> beyond the vomiting dark,
> beyond the stomach walls
> of the shark.
>   (141)

This passage reveals the power of interpretative line division and the influence of sound, sense, and sight. The repetition and rhyme of *gnaws;* the dissonance of the *a* sounds in the three *gnaws* and of the alliterative *sheet steel scrap* as well as the sharp blow effect of the six monosyllabic words in line two; the emphasis on *way* and *beyond* through repetition; the connotative imagery in all its factual horror; the word function and the dramatic pause which determine the length of line—all explain the effectiveness of Hideho's story of the "black" sea turtle and the "white" shark.

Hideho concludes the section with a metaphoric description of the birth of a work of art. He compares the artist to a woman in labor, whose baby is the art work. In the Kingdom of Poetry, the travail may last for years; and there are many abortions as a result of quacks. The "Eddie Jests and Shortfellows" use no contraceptives as they copulate "with muses on the wrong side of the tracks." And many famous or successful poets abandon the little "hybrid bastards of their youth" (144) without even bidding them farewell.

In "Chi" the Curator analyzes the "bifacial nature" of Hideho's poetry. He discovers that Hideho writes not only the "racial ballad in the public domain" but also "the private poem in the modern vein" (145)—just as Tolson himself did. Hideho once admitted to the Curator the fear that he would be just another statistic when he died—unless his poetry lived. The Curator understands Hideho's dilemma: "to be or not to be/a Negro" (146). When the Curator takes Hideho, who is in a drunken stupor, home one night, he sees one of his modern poems, "E. & O.E." (the title of one of Tolson's earlier poems). In the poem the Curator reads Hideho's argument with himself:

> Why place an empty pail
> before a well
> of dry bones?
> Why go to Nineveh to tell
> the ailing that they ail?
> Why lose a golden fleece
> to gain a holy grail?
>   (147)

Hideho, the hero of the black masses, ridicules the artist or leader who does "Uncle Tom's asinine splits" (148). Why should the poet give up his position as *Coeur de Lion* for what might well be an empty dream? The Curator's appetite was whetted as he read more of the poem which was so unlike the popular ballads the Harlem Gallery patrons applauded:

> Beneath
> the albatross,
> the skull-and-bones
> the Skull and Cross,
> the Seven Sins Dialectical,
> I do not shake

the Wailing Wall
of Earth—
nor quake
the Gethsemane
of Sea—
nor tear
the Big Top
of Sky
with Lear's prayer
or Barabas' curse
or Job's cry!
(151)

In the penultimate section, "Psi," the Curator pulls together what he has set forth in this "autobio-fragment." Much has been left undone, he admits, but he has faced the problems of the black artist. His controversial work pulses with black characters and with philosophics unacceptable to a considerable segment of both the white and the black reading public, and it is written in a difficult style, which limits his audience. To be a black artist is to be "a flower of the gods, whose growth/is dwarfed at an early stage—" (153) by both black and white critics. Yet, his artistic integrity is intact, and, as Doctor Nkomo has said, *"What* is he" who has no self-respect? (153).

The Curator muses about those who have tried unsuccessfully to destroy the self-respect of the black man; and he thinks, ironically, that Nature, at least, has played fair with the African: she has given him a "fleecy canopy" to protect his brain from the sun; a dark skin for work or play; an "accommodation nose" that cools the hot air; an "epidermis in broils" on which "lice infested" hair will not grow. "Black Boy" must not become discouraged with his plight in America; he must realize that a grapevine from Bordeaux planted elsewhere will not produce Bordeaux wine; and he must beware of believing every wine label that he reads. Of one thing he can be certain: that "every people, by and by, produces its 'Château Bottled'" (159).

Again the Curator asks the difficult question "Who is a Negro?" The Curator himself passes for white in Norfolk, but he is a black man in New York. His years of experience as a black American have caused him to conclude that, even though the White World may have an arctic attitude, black and white must learn to work

and live together: "you [the white man] are the wick that absorbs
the oil in my lamp,/in all kinds of weather;/and we are teeth in
the pitch wheel [19] that work together" (161). He continues to reflect on the Afro-American—he is "a dish in the white man's
kitchen—/a potpourri," a dish nobody knows. The mixture of
bloods resulting from "midnight-to-dawn lecheries,/in cabin and
big house" (162,163) have produced all shades of white, black,
and in-between. The Curator concludes the section by prophesy-
ing the eventual mixture of the black and white races, despite
the ugly past and overwhelming obstacles that lie ahead:

> In a Vision in a Dream,
> from the frigid seaport of the proud Xanthochroid,
> the good ship Défineznegro
> sailed fine, under an unabridged moon,
> to reach the archipelago
> Nigeridentité.
> In the Strait of Octoroon,
> off black Scylla,
> after the typhoon Phobos, out of the Stereotypus Sea,
> had rived her hull and sail to a T,
> the Défineznegro sank the rock
> and disappeared in the abyss
> (Vanitas vanitatum!)
> of white Charybdis.
>
> (164)

"Omega," the final book, addresses both "White Boy" and
"Black Boy" as the Curator recapitulates the ideas presented
throughout Harlem Gallery. He says that even a person caught in
the trap of environment may "luck" upon "the know-how of a rac-
coon/that gnaws off its leg to escape from a trap" (165). Though
the Curator has no doctor of philosophy degree from Harvard, as
some do, those so fortunate may not have learned how to loosen,
as he has, whatever "ball and chain" they drag around. The artist
must be strong, for his integrity is constantly tested. He has difficult decisions to make: Will he stand on his head in the middle of
Main Street to get coins from the vulgar? Will he paint an "ignus
fatuus of nawiht" to win the approval of the elite? And why
should it be a sin for a "chef d'oeuvre" to be esoteric? Should man
not imitate his Master? The Curator gives Tolson's answer to

those who would attack his intellectual style when he asks if he should "skim the milk of culture for the elite/and give the 'lesser breeds' a popular latex brand" (167), or if he should simplify his work to "increase digestibility." He states that it is the imagination of the artist which finally "steers the work of art aright" (167). The Curator, like Tolson, insists that what the artist must have above all else is freedom—his oxygen. Ever concerned about artistic freedom, among his notes, Tolson jotted, "We're not concerned with what school the poet belongs to; only how good is the poem he writes. A poet, like a student, has the inalienable right to select his school." [20]

Harlem Gallery concludes on the personal, intimate tone with which it began when it awoke the Curator "at a people's dusk of dawn." What the Curator has done is to paint "dramatis personae in the dusk of dawn,/between America's epigraph and epitaph" (171). At times, the "millstones of the Regents" have ground the Curator's spirit almost away, but he has kept at his long task of envisioning the Harlem Gallery of his people; for he knows that "The present is only intelligible in the light of the past" (171). Now that the Curator's literary work is completed, he expects to hear no "Selika's invisible choir" singing of the "Beyond's equalizing bar" (172). If this work should be celebrated, the author would be unprepared for the deluge. Nor would he have the means whereby to defy the "dusky Regents," who "can knot the golden purse strings/while closeted in the Great Amen,/and mix the ingredients of Syncorax' brew!" (173).

One final riddle—perhaps a warning or prophecy—the Curator leaves with the reader: in the America of the 1960's, with its racial division, although the white heather and white almond (symbols of life) grow in the black ghetto, the hyacinth and asphodel (symbols of death) blow in the white metropolis. As for his *Harlem Gallery*, though the public may have an "arctic rigidity" in art, the Curator hazards that his work is "no chippy fire"; "for here, in focus, are paintings that chronicle/a people's New World odyssey/from chattel to Esquire!" (173).

IX   *Reviews of* Harlem Gallery

When Karl Shapiro hailed Tolson as "one of the great architects of modern poetry" and indicted the poetic establishment for ignoring him for years because he was a black poet, he invited a diversity of critical reaction. Indeed, one reviewer wrote, that "Mr. Shapiro's praise of *Harlem Gallery* is so high that it starts the reader off with an adverse reaction: 'Oh, look now. It can't be that good.' " [21]

Laurence Lieberman quarrels with Shapiro's statement that "*Tolson writes in Negro*," claiming that many of his black students at St. Thomas come from diverse parts of the world and are both intelligent and interested in poetry, yet they do not understand Tolson. How, then, he claims, can Shapiro say "Tolson writes in *Negro?*" [22] Sarah Webster Fabio, black poet and critic, also says that Shapiro's "identification of Tolson's language as being authentically 'Negro' is a gross inaccuracy"; and she names instead such black writers and artists as Paul Laurence Dunbar, Phyllis Wheatley, Bessie Smith, Mahalia Jackson, Ray Charles, Willie Mae Thornton, Langston Hughes, and LeRoi Jones, who, she writes, come "to a lyric with a widely diverse body of diction and still, I think, speak 'Negro.' " [23] Whether or not Lieberman and Miss Fabio rightfully interpret Shapiro's statement can be pursued by reading an article by Shapiro which appears in the *Wilson Library Bulletin* in which he elaborates upon his controversial statement about Tolson.[24] As Shapiro suspected, several critics also challenged his statement that the reason for the limited size of Tolson's audience is that he is a black poet.[25]

Most critics comment on Tolson's style, about which they usually have a strong feeling one way or the other; but some also seem to quarrel even with their own opinions. For instance, Lieberman says the book is "top-heavy" with tradition, special learning, and literary allusions; and he objects to passages "cluttered" with references to artists and their works; yet he writes that *Harlem Gallery* has "astonishing linguistic range, a vital new imagery and much technical excitement." [26] To an Australian reviewer, Tolson writes "as an academic gone underground"; and he considers his "outpounding of Pound," which Shapiro emphasized, a flaw.[27] David Littlejohn also finds *Harlem Gallery* "clogged" with literary allusions, which he refers to as Tolson's "strange difficulties." [28]

On the other hand, a London *Times* reviewer writes that, although the work is difficult in the tradition of Pound, Eliot, and Hart Crane, "the artificially created idiom is itself the poem's theme: the nature of Negro art in a white culture. . . ." [29] Though most critics immediately place Tolson in the Eliot-Pound school, Tolson regarded himself as more closely related to Hart Crane than to either Pound or Eliot. In the light of a comment by David Daiches concerning the limitations of Eliot's influence— "There is, in fact, however much Mr. Eliot may repudiate personality in poetry, a highly idiosyncratic personality at work here whose solutions of common problems are *not* really helpful to others, for all the influence of his merely technical procedures on younger poets. . . ." [30]—one might wonder if the conclusion that Eliot exerted an overabundant influence on Tolson might not result from a somewhat superficial reading. Robert Donald Spector, in an article which appeared in *Saturday Review*, expressed little concern about Eliot's influence on Tolson—instead, he emphasizes Tolson's originality and artistry in *Harlem Gallery:* "But what of the fantastic way in which discussions of esthetics are turned into social comment? What of tho incredible manner in which Tolson ranges over every field of art, plays adroitly with the language? These require pages of demonstration. Sufficient to say that whatever his reputation in the present critical climate, Tolson stands firmly as a great American poet." [31]

In *Harlem Gallery* Tolson manipulates skillfully the tools he has been readying for many years. The metaphorical language, the symbolism, characterization, philosophical dialogue, his "S-trilogy," climax, the strong sense of grammar—all of these serve him well in what he considered his best work. The reviews indicate that *Harlem Gallery* is something of an enigma to many readers, but they recognize it as a work which must be reckoned with. *How* to approach it critically is the question; for it is, in the words of one British critic, a "strangely isolated work." [32]

Chapter 5 takes up the question of evaluation, as well as the attendant problem of categorizing Tolson, who is a black poet—a point which he always emphasized; an American poet; and, in his all-embracing concern for mankind and his ability to make the black man's experience a concern of all, a universalist.

CHAPTER *5*

Tolson's Place in Literature

I judge
My soul
Eagle
Nor mole:
A man
Is what
He saves
From rot.
—Tolson, *Rendezvous with America*

IN the introduction to *Harlem Gallery,* Karl Shapiro poses a challenge to all those who would evaluate Tolson's work:

> It is not enough to equate Tolson, as his best critics have done, with Eliot or Hart Crane, the CANTOS or ANABASE. To make him equal is to miss the point, just as it would be to make him *better than.* Tolson writes and thinks in Negro, which is to say, a possible American language. He is therefore performing the primary poetic rite for our literature. Instead of purifying the tongue, which is the business of the Academy, he is complicating it, giving it the gift of tongues. Pound, Eliot, and Joyce did this; but with a pernicious nostalgia that all but killed the patient. Tolson does it naturally and to the manner born.[1]

More attention has been paid to Shapiro's statement that "Tolson writes and thinks in Negro" than to any other; for, while some few critics agree, more of them—both black and white—have, as has been stated, challenged Shapiro's assertion. The crux of Shapiro's comments, however, is the difficulty, or rather the impossibility, of putting Tolson's poetry on an evaluative scale with that of other poets; for Tolson's poetry is unique. Stylistically, he is akin to T. S. Eliot, Ezra Pound, and Hart Crane; but, in content, they are quite different, as he pointed out in a letter to a friend in 1961: "My work is certainly difficult in metaphors, symbols, and juxtaposed ideas. There the similarity between Eliot and me separates . . . when you look at my ideas and Eliot's, we're as far apart as hell and heaven." [2] Like most black poets today, Tolson found his material in his people; and he celebrates their blackness. Yet, because his style is quite foreign to that of other black poets— including those who express themselves often in an intellectual, symbolic vein, such as Gwendolyn Brooks, Robert Hayden, and LeRoi Jones—it is difficult to compare Tolson's work with theirs.

I *Tolson and the Black Esthetic*

At the time of Tolson's death in 1966, the movement toward a Black Esthetic was beginning to gain momentum. This separatist movement would undoubtedly have had his sympathy in many of its manifestations, for Tolson understood all too well the frustration which had conceived it. His vision for America, however, was never a separation of peoples but a multiracial culture composed of many kinds of American artists, each preserving the qualities of his particular race for the enlightenment and appreciation of all men. Because of this broad concept of the role of the black artist and its application in his own work, it is understandable that his work, which obviously was not written for the average reader— black or white—is not considered of importance at the present time by many adherents of the Black Consciousness Movement.

In a review of an anthology of black poetry, *Kaleidoscope,* edited by black poet Robert Hayden, Don Lee, a popular young black poet, dismisses Tolson in one sentence: "Melvin B. Tolson is represented with some of his less obscure poetry which still exhibits his range and his capacity to lose the people that may read him." [3] Ironically, an article highlighting the work of Lee as black writer-in-residence at Cornell University at the time includes a quotation from Tolson's "The Poet" to delineate the role of Lee as a leader in the Black Esthetic Movement:

> A Champion of the People versus Kings—
> His only martyrdom is poetry:
> A hater of the hierarchy of things—
> Freedom's need is his necessity.[4]

Shortly after Tolson's poem quoted above had appeared in *Rendezvous with America* a quarter of a century earlier, a reviewer had quoted the same lines and had applied them to their author: "Tolson is what he declares of fellow singers in 'The Poet,' 'A champion of the People versus Kings. . . .'"[5]

In Lee's review of *Kaleidoscope*, Tolson fares well, however, compared to Robert Hayden, a widely known black poet of whose "belligerent ignorance" Lee writes because Hayden refers to black poets as *Negro*, a term now considered derogatery by many black Americans. Hayden, he writes, is one of those black poets who perpetuates the "very dangerous myth" that poets other than black poets or critics are qualified to judge black poetry:

> I believe that this is an absurdity to say the least; how can one who is not a part of our culture, a part of our immediate life, a part of us, judge us? How can they, WASP, have a proper perspective to work from? If there is to be judgment, then we, as Afro-Americans, are better prepared to pass judgment on them. We blacks have a much wider perspective to work from for we are the products of a dual culture, *ie.*, Shakespeare during the day and LeRoi Jones at night, or Americanism during the day and survival at night.[6]

Lee's comments set forth one of the chief tenets of the Black Esthetic Movement: the black writer should write for black readers, who alone are qualified to judge his work. He apparently dismisses Tolson because of his intellectualism—"his capacity to lose the people that may read him." Of course, this accusation was one Tolson had lived with since turning to the modernist idiom in the 1950's. His decision to develop this difficult and challenging style, which, in Shapiro's judgment, he does "naturally and to the manner born," would limit his "horizontal audience," would be the object of criticism for some, and would cause him to be ignored by others as too difficult to bother with; but, when he realized that it was the technique with which he could work best artistically, he had no other choice.

And so Tolson fortified himself for the adverse, sometimes cruel, criticism of men like Paul Breman, who wrote after Tolson's death that he "postured for a white audience, and with a wicked sense of humour gave it just what it wanted: an entertaining darkey using almost comically big words as the best wasp tradition demands of its educated house-niggers." [7] But Tolson, like the Curator in *Harlem Gallery*, was "a *strange* bird—/a jacobin of horny, reversed epidermal outgrowths" (119), who could catch "a twenty-pound, round/solid missile fired from a cannon/thirty feet away" (120). And he prepared an answer to such criticism in "Omega," the concluding section of *Harlem Gallery*, as the Curator, who speaks here for Tolson, asks, as has been pointed out in Chapter 4,

> Should he
> skim the milk of culture for the elite
> and give the "lesser breeds"
> a popular latex brand?
> Should he
> (to increase digestibility)
> break up
> the fat globules and vitamins and casein shreds?
>   (167)

For the artist, the Curator says, there can be only one answer:

> Tonic spasms of wind and wave
> assail compass and lamp in the cabined night;
> but the binnacle of the imagination
> steers the work of art aright—
>   (167)

The Curator continues his defense by saying that, if this intellectual style be found wanting, his only answer is that the artist must be free to excel in whatever way his imagination directs him; for above all else, the artist, as has been noted, must have freedom. And Tolson, through the Curator, adds: why should an artist not strive to reach the highest goal of which he is artistically capable?

> White Boy,
> Black Boy,
> freedom is the oxygen
> of the studio and gallery.
> What if a *chef-d'oeuvre* is esoteric?
> The cavernous By Room, with its unassignable variety
> of ego-dwarfing
> stalactites and stalagmites,

> makes my veins and arteries vibrate faster
> as I study its magnificence and intricacy.
>   Is it amiss or odd
>   if the apes of God
>   take a cue from their Master?
>   (169)

Sarah Webster Fabio, a black critic, accuses Tolson of cultivating a "vast, bizarre, pseudo-literary diction" to meet the demands of the Establishment when many other black poets were abandoning Pound and Eliot to meet the needs of their race.[8] In like manner, Don Lee castigates all black writers who worry about being judged and criticized and therefore inevitably write for "critics, for WASP, for National Book Awards" (a direct attack on Ralph Ellison). To Lee, the black poet must set the literary standards for his time, which he cannot do by "prostituting" himself for critics or imitating other poets.[9]

Miss Fabio and Lee do not, of course, represent the thinking of all black critics. Clinton Oliver of Queens College, Flushing, New York, whose doctoral dissertation at Harvard was "The Name and Nature of American Negro Literature," comments about Miss Fabio's criticism of Tolson:

> Tolson is one of our major voices. This is criticism brought not
> only against Tolson but against Ellison, and it dismisses the rich-
> ness of Western Tradition. It is too simplistic. Africans do not dis-
> card French culture. They build upon it. The New Breed following
> LeRoi Jones forgets Dante's influence on him. DuBois too used
> techniques he learned at Harvard and in Germany and applied
> them to his people. I think *Harlem Gallery* is one of the great
> works of its time.[10]

Neither does Saunders Redding, black author and critic, see any future, at least in America, for that school of black writers which seeks to establish a "black aesthetic." To Redding, "aesthetics has no racial, national or geographical boundaries. Beauty and truth, the principal components of aesthetics, are universal."[11] This conservative attitude is not limited to the older black writers, although most of the young writers favor the Black Consciousness Movement. Alice Walker, a young Georgia writer, sounds much like T. S. Eliot or William Butler Yeats when she says that black writers should direct their work toward an "imaginary ideal audience that will appreciate what they have to say, and profit from it." To her, "it is only important that we write from within ourselves and that we direct our efforts outward. Period. I would have liked for Victor Hugo to like my stories quite as much as I admire his." [12] These contrasting attitudes of black writers and critics make clear the dichotomy of opinion which exists among them today.

II *Tolson's Stance as a Black Poet*

Though Tolson is presently accused by some black critics of catering stylistically to the white Establishment's demands, he was considered during his lifetime one of the most outspoken "radicals" in the Civil Rights Movement. His longtime friend and fellow writer Arna Bontemps has asserted that Tolson had the courage to "carry the ball" in an era when such courage was rarely demonstrated openly. [13] Had the hundreds of hours he dedicated to giving speeches on the rights of black Americans and had the energy he expended in teaching and inspiring countless black students that they could, by hard work, compete with graduates from Ivy League colleges or anywhere else gone into the writing of poetry, his literary output would have been far more substantial than it is. The theme of almost all of his poetry is his people; but he chose, instead of addressing himself only to a black audience, to use the black man as a symbol of all who are oppressed and who seek the freedom which is rightfully theirs, thus raising his people through his poetry to a universal level.

The courage Tolson exemplified when he dared the wrath of southern whites to preach his message of hope and human rights is the same courage he embodies as a poet. In his poetry he is just as outspoken concerning the injustices meted out to the underprivileged as he had been in those midnight speeches in South Texas in the 1920's and 1930's. Believing that the poet must have the "oxygen of freedom" to create beauty and truth as he sees it, he dared to satirize not only the tyranny of the whites but the hypocrisies of the "Black Bourgeoisie"; and he discovered beauty in lowbrow black society at a time when many black people wished to ignore this subject. What some of his critics seem to overlook is that, at the time Tolson wrote, the criterion for art was that of the "Great White World," which meant that a black poet whose objective was to show the whole world that he, as a representative of black people, could write as well as any other poet, had to compete in the only frame of reference available. He could, of course, have directed his poetry, as Langston Hughes and many other black writers did, to black readers primarily; but Tolson made the choice which he believed would be most meaningful in years to come both for him and his people—knowing full well that his choice would be misinterpreted and maligned by some. Whether or not he made the right choice—whether or not, as Miss Fabio suggests, Pound is "out" permanently and Tolson with him —only time will tell.

Tolson came to realize, like Yeats, that his reputation would never be established in his lifetime by his people; but he believed the most valuable contribution he could make to his race was to achieve a high level of artistry with black materials and, in doing so, not to limit his audience to his people. Tolson was a master teacher—and he wanted to educate the world in a subject which he felt had too long been omitted from its curriculum—the black man. Abraham Chapman, editor of a recent anthology of black literature, *Black Voices,* points out the affinity of Yeats to the best black writers:

> In his poetic approach, Yeats united three components which to others may seem irreconcilable or incompatible: to express the personal and private self, to express the common humanity the individual shares with all men—and to express the ethnic or racial self with its particular mythology and cultural past. If for "Irishry" we substitute black or Negro consciousness we can see that the best of the Afro-American writers have been struggling to express and blend the three components Yeats speaks of and a fourth as well, which has made the situation of the black writer in America even more complex: their personal selves, their universal humanity, the peculiar qualities and beauty of their blackness and ethnic specificity, and their American selves. These are not separate and boxed-off compartments of the mind and soul, but the inseparable and intermingled elements of a total human being, of a whole person who blends diversities within himself. This is the rich blend we find in the best of the Negro American artists.[14]

This description fits Tolson well in its application to all three of his books of poetry, for from them all emanate Tolson, the man;

Tolson, a part of mankind; Tolson, a black man; and Tolson, an American.

Though Tolson's work has been criticized adversely by some black writers and ignored by others, there are those who are very much aware of the contribution he has made to contemporary literature. Gwendolyn Brooks, the only black poet to be awarded the Pulitzer Prize (1950), supports the Black Esthetic; but she said that, in her opinion, Tolson should have been given the Pulitzer Prize for *Harlem Gallery*.[15] James A. Emmanuel and Theodore Gross, editors of *Dark Symphony*—a recent anthology of black literature (1968), named for Tolson's poem "Dark Symphony" published some twenty-four years previously—when writing of the "startling waywardness of the poet's genius," prophesy that Tolson's contribution "to the Negro tradition in American poetry, merging high-blown intellectualism with 'ham, hocks, ribs, and jowls' straight from Harlem, is secure." [16] In *The Negro History Bulletin*, Dolphin G. Thompson points out that Tolson "demonstrated a superb poetic talent in *Rendezvous*," that *Libretto* "struck with hurricane force in the citadel of letters" and was promptly "consigned to death in a conspiracy of silence," which he blames on "artistic jealousy and shame"; and that Tolson has a significant place in world literature. Thompson describes *Harlem Gallery* in these words: "He [Tolson] has taken the language of American and the idiom of the world to fashion a heroic declaration of, about, and for the Negro in America. It is a book that should be on every bookshelf. . . . In addition to mastering poetic techniques he has initiated a style of dramatically lifting the Negro experience to a classical grace." [17] And, more recently, J. A. Ramsaran has hailed Tolson, along with Aimé Césaire and E. R. Braithwaite, as a poet whose work reveals a "return to Africa in a spiritual sense." He says that in *Harlem Gallery*, Tolson, "with masterly mordent [*sic*] irony—classifies, arranges and juxtaposes Black, white, and all the shades between" as he "moves toward a synthesis of the Afro-American experience with its manifold strands of race and cultures. . . ." [18]

III *Art versus Life*

When Tolson learned that he had cancer, his fear was that his life would end before he could complete his five-volume epic

poem and establish himself as a major twentieth-century poet—
and one remembers the fear of Hideho Heights in *Harlem Gallery*
that if he died with no poems "in World Lit—he'd be a statistic!"
Though Tolson had suffered many discouraging moments with rejection slips and frustrations of various types in his more than fifty
years as a writer, he had never doubted that he could carve a
permanent niche for himself as a poet whose work would long
outlive him and his contemporaries. When he completed *Harlem
Gallery: Book I, The Curator,* he felt secure in his technique and
with his subject matter. He no longer searched for a style as he
had after the publication of *Rendezvous;* and he did not feel
"written out" as he had when he had finished *Libretto.* But now
that he had the time, which was all he needed to complete his
work, the good health which he had enjoyed throughout his life
was denied him—another Hardeian quirk of fate.

Many poets have produced far more in shorter lifetimes, but
Melvin Tolson was a man with many interests, many talents, and
many demands on his time. Mrs. Tolson has said often that, if her
husband had chosen to put his work before his family, as many
writers have done, he could have developed the style of his maturity much sooner and have published far more than he did; but
more important to Tolson than even his writing was his dream for
his family—a dream which perhaps only a black American can
fully appreciate. This dream was fulfilled when he saw his wife
and daughter receive master's degrees and his three sons awarded
doctor of philosophy degrees. Not only did Tolson inspire his family to attain excellent educations; he poured all of his energy into
whatever task was at hand. When he taught, he never sat at his
desk as he lectured; his voice boomed out as he paced up and
down, using his whole body forcefully to convey his meaning.
Shortly after his return to the classroom following his second operation for cancer, he appalled his students when he demonstrated some point by running up and down the elevated tiers in
the classroom. When he taught at Wiley College, he traveled
thousands of miles with his debate teams, going on the faith that
they would draw large enough crowds to meet their expenses, setting records wherever they went. When he turned from debate to
drama, he built excellent dramatic programs at Wiley and later at
Langston University, where he founded the Dust Bowl Players. A

letter to "The Contributors' Column" of the *Atlantic Monthly* in 1941 describes some of his activities at Wiley College:

> At the present time I am trying to build, on our campus, the Log Cabin School of Drama and Speech. An ex-slave has given us several acres of timber; a white plumber and four Negro carpenters are giving their services; a white printer is getting out the propaganda; and in general, the boys and girls are scouring the regions with the collection boxes. We aren't discouraged, for we've covered thousands of miles on our debate and drama tours with bad brakes, bad motors, bad tires, and bad drivers. Give us time, and we'll have Negro theatres springing up in cotton patches! We'll take what we have and make what we want.[19]

This was Tolson—no matter what the task. Although the theater was never completed, the project took much of his writing time. As Melvin, Jr., has observed, "When I consider how many different things Dad did, how completely he gave himself to whatever he did, the question that comes to my mind is not 'Why did he write so little?' but 'How did he write so much?' "[20] Tolson had an abundance of talents and the inability to say "No" when he was called upon. To shut himself off from his family and friends was not living for him. He loved people with a vigor noticeable even to those who knew him only briefly. A novelist who had talked with him two or three times paid this tribute to him shortly after his death:

> Tolson's life was devoted to . . . a belief in the essential sameness of men, and their common need for a decent chance to grow. As he himself grew as a poet, he became a clear, strong voice for friendship and love. . . . If Tolson had any quality that was most impressive, it was his uncanny ability to make every person he met feel special—important. He was a superbly successful human being whose love for his fellow men gave him a vitality unique in my experience.[21]

Again that word *unique*—Tolson was a unique person as well as a unique poet. Testimonials to his involvement with people appear among his papers in the form of dozens of requests from those who called on him for guidance and help: letters asking him to appear as achievement day vespers speaker at Grambling College in Louisiana; to judge speech contests both on the high school and college level; to be commencement speaker in Amarillo, Texas, and in many other towns; to send suggestions and planning methods for teaching a course in journalism; to offer a correspondence course in the art of letter writing; to criticize poems by budding poets; to recommend former students for various positions; even to send the writer the name of the person Figaro married in *The Marriage of Figaro*. Among his notes also are the "Five Steps of a Man": (1) the nonhuman or feral; (2) the human; (3) the humane; (4) the humanistic; (5) the humanitarian. Tolson was a humanitarian, a man concerned with the welfare of all men. The decisions Tolson made throughout his life indicate that, when he was forced to choose between being a productive poet and sharing a warm relationship with his fellow man, his poetry came second.

IV   Final Judge: The "Vertical" Audience

Though a divided opinion exists about Tolson's work among both black and white critics because of its undeniable difficulty, its limited quantity, and its candid criticism of various large segments of American society, it is a contribution which cannot be ignored. Emmanuel and Gross predict that the immediate future of his reputation may depend upon the rise of black critics and their attitude toward the new "Black Esthetic," [22] but Tolson was never so concerned about the present or immediate future as about the long-range picture. At this time, *Harlem Gallery* is seven years old, and Shapiro's words about *Libretto* twelve years after its publication are applicable to *Harlem Gallery* today: it "speaks for itself. . . . Possibly it is too early for the assimilation of such a poem, even by poets." [23]

Tolson's work marks him as an esoteric poet whose poetry, though it is contained in only three volumes, offers a wealth of material for critics to consider for years to come. One indication that his star is rising is the decision of Collier Publishing Company to publish his books in paperback. *Harlem Gallery* is now available, and the publication of *Rendezvous*, the most readable for the general public of the three, will put it in print for the first time in over twenty years, which should increase his reading public considerably.

Tolson's poetry has also been brought to public attention through the musical composition of T. J. Anderson, a former colleague of Tolson's at Langston University who is now composer-in-residence with the Atlantic Symphony Orchestra. On May 26, 1970, Anderson conducted in the Atlanta Memorial Arts Center as a part of a program presented under a grant from the National Endowment for the Arts, Washington, D.C., the premiere performance of his "Variations on a Theme by M. B. Tolson"—a work which juxtaposes excerpts from *Libretto* and *Harlem Gallery* as text and which is written for soprano, violin, cello, alto saxophone, trumpet, trombone, and piano:

Variations on a Theme by

M. B. Tolson

Words by M. B. Tolson excerpted from

*Harlem Gallery: **Libretto for the
Book I, The Curator   and   Republic of Liberia

*The Harlem Gallery, an Afric pepper bird
awakes me at a people's dusk of dawn.
The age alters [sic] its image, a dog's hind leg,
and hazards the moment of truth in pawn.
The Lord of the House of Flies,
jaundice-eyed, synapses purled,
wries before the tumultous canvas,
The Second of May—
by Goya:
the dagger of Madrid
vs.
the scimitar of Murat.
In Africa, in Asia, on the Day
of Barricades, alarm birds bedevil the Great White World,
a Buridan's ass—not Balaam's—between no oats and hay.

** "It is the grass that suffers when
two elephants fight. The white man solves
between white sheets his black

"problem. Where would the rich cream be
without skim milk? The eye can cross the
river in a flood."

*Dr. Nkomo says: "The little python would not let go
the ass of the frog—so the big python swallowed both."
I seem to sense behind the mask of the Zulu Club Wits
thoughts springing clear of
the *terra firma* of the mind—
the mettled forelegs of horses
in a curvet.

** "A stinkbug should not peddle perfume.
The tide that ebbs will flow again.
A louse that bites is in
"the inner shirt. An open door
sees both inside and out. The saw
that severs the topmost limb
"comes from the ground."

** A fabulous mosaic log,
the Bola boa lies
gorged to the hinges of his jaws,
eyeless, yet with eyes . . .

in the interlude of peace.

The beaked and pouched assassin sags
on to his corsair rock,
and from his talons swim the blood—
red feathers of a cock . . .

in the interlude of peace.

The tawny typhoon striped with black
torpors in grasses tan:
a doomsday cross, his paws uprear
the leveled skull of a man . . .

in the interlude of peace.

*Come back, Baby, come back—I need your gravy.
Come back, Baby, come back—I'm weak and wavy.
The talk of the town, I'm Skid Row bound—
and I don't mean maybe!

These excerpts (the text) were printed on the chamber concert
program. An Atlanta *Journal* music critic called the work "excellent" and commented that "the fragmentation of the music reflects
the same quality in the text," causing an "undeniable effect—ironic,
tense, angry, occasionally despairing." [24] A reviewer for the Atlan-

tic *Constitution* called soprano Bernadine Oliphant's rendition of the text "haunting" and described the work as "important . . . both for its music and for its theme"—the "agonized outcry apparently induced by the situation of the black man in the world today." [25] One indication of the impact of this work is the fact that it was presented in the Library of Congress on March 24, 1972.

What exactly then is the contribution Tolson has made to contemporary literature? First, *Rendezvous* contains several excellent poems which are being recognized more each year by editors of anthologies. Although few of Tolson's poems have been set to music, *Rendezvous* contains many lyrical lines which would lend themselves to a musical background, such as certain sections of "Dark Symphony," as well as "Ballad of the Rattlesnake" with its up-to-date theme of racial frustration, hatred, violence, revenge, and the consequences. In *Libretto*, Tolson has taught the history of the courageous little African republic in symbolic, allusive language; but he also shows the motives of those who originated the idea of founding Liberia, the first "victims" who established the colony, the greedy nations who fed on its narrowing boundaries— all in the impressive intellectual style which was his trademark from this time on.

In *Harlem Gallery*, he succeeded in creating, through representative types, dramatic scenes, and philosophical discussions, a community of black Americans who offer an education to all who meet them in the one hundred and seventy-three pages of their existence. In this book, his style is somewhat relaxed in comparison with *Libretto*—though it is also intellectually stimulating and challenging. In much of *Harlem Gallery* he employs the dramatic scene, which he enjoyed writing and wrote effectively. A former dramatist, Tolson, like Frost, had "a great love of people and of talk." Tolson ranges easily from the level of intellectual word play on down. The allusions and special learning are still there, but the sometimes strained quality of *Libretto* is gone. In this work, Tolson truly found his voice as he juxtaposed the literary and literal worlds in which he lived.

These three works contain many memorable lines, as well as a number of unforgettable characters. Tolson teaches by satirizing the shortcomings of both "saints" and "sinners." He says of the artist in one of his many notes on the subject that he magnifies life in order to make people recognize themselves: "If you don't want to see life pictured on the stage, on the canvas, in a book, then clean up the vulgarity and vice in your own house, in your own town, in your own country. . . . After all, the artist is the mirror that reflects life as it is. The artist does not make life; he pictures life. . . ." Tolson studied intensely the English language and world literatures, and he made use of his vast knowledge in his poetry. As Melvin, Jr., has remarked, "Dad realized that all English belonged to him and he used it in the way an orchestra leader uses music when he conducts." [26] He served his apprenticeship as a stylist by studying the developers of the New Poetry of the early twentieth century, but his style was guided primarily by his "three S's of Parnassus"—sight, sound, and sense. And those who have heard Tolson lecture or engaged him in conversation recognize his poetic style as his own—not as a weak imitation of anyone.

Perhaps the chief handicap in Tolson's style lies not in any inability on his part but in the fact that, by the time he had developed it, the poets who had introduced the stress on intellectualism, symbolism, and allusion had abandoned in large part these techniques. As early as 1917, Eliot spoke of recovering "the accents of direct speech" in poetry; and he wrote again in 1942 that "the task is to explore the musical possibilities of an established convention of the relation of the idiom of verse to that of speech; at other periods the task is to catch up with the changes of colloquial speech." [27] Robert Frost succeeded in making poetry out of conversation; and as early as 1913 Yeats said that he tried to make his work convincing with "a speech so natural and dramatic that the hearer would feel the presence of man thinking and feeling." [28]

Certainly Tolson was aware of the change which Eliot, Yeats, and the other poets whom he read closely had made, but he could not abandon the style in which he had discovered he could best express himself. If this style was outmoded, it would not exclude him from his place among twentieth-century poets, he believed; for the true artist writes for the future. Karl Shapiro does not mention Tolson by name in his book entitled A Primer for Poets (1953), but his description of the way the poet develops his style describes well the way Tolson developed his technique: "It is not that the poet achieves style as a highjumper achieves height, as much as it is that he achieves selfhood and personality. . . . The poet's artifice consists in making his lines conform to the degree of change he has experienced. The alterations he makes time and time and again in a single phrase or a single word are not for 'effects'; they are a search for the exact degree of change which he has lived and which is a part of him." [29]

Tolson's style, as has been indicated, was a part of Tolson. Though he was a "gentle and warm man who wore his vast erudition lightly," [30] as Herbert Hill said of him in a memorial column, he *was* an erudite person, as the style he preferred reveals. There is no question, of course, that at times he is overzealous in pursuing a metaphor or an alliterative, onomatopoetic line which becomes forced and artificial rather than poetic, as in parts of *Libretto:* and it is obvious that he tried too hard to "make every line a great one." [31]

Had Tolson completed the five-volume epic poem of *Harlem Gallery* relating the story of the black man in America, and had he sustained the caliber of Volume I, *The Curator*, he would have accomplished one of the most extraordinary feats of any poet in the twentieth century. Like other writers of excellence whom death has claimed at their zenith, he has nevertheless attained a high place in contemporary literature. As has been noted, his uniqueness makes it difficult, if not impossible, to put him on a rating scale with other poets, black or white. Without doubt, he stands as one of the best black poets in America; and his unique and outstanding contribution to American literature should be recognized by the inclusion of his poetry in any anthology of twentieth-century American literature.

Tolson's decision to sacrifice quantity for quality, and, when necessary, art for life, was in keeping with the integrity he maintained as artist and as a man—despite pressures of various kinds. As he lay in St. Paul's Hospital in Dallas during that last long summer of 1966, he said that he had no regrets—he was a happy man.[32] His family had the security of good educations; and, though there had been numerous temptations, he had kept the faith as artist—like John Laugart in *Harlem Gallery,* he had never sold "mohair for alpaca/to ring the bell!" (41); as a man, his greatest compensation was that he "had more beds to sleep in and more invitations to dinner" than he could ever find time to accept. He would have been pleased with the tribute which appeared in an Oklahoma City newspaper shortly after his death: "he was a superbly successful human being." [33]

His sensitivity as a black poet dictated the subjects and themes of his work; his artistic imagination and intellect determined his technique. He had done what he had to do. There are those who find fault with his work; but there are many who agree with Spector, Shapiro, and others who say that, regardless of his reputation in the "present critical climate," he stands "firmly as a great American poet." [34] The final evaluation of his contribution as a poet will be determined in years to come by that "vertical audience" for which he wrote—by both black and white scholars who have scarcely penetrated the surface of the complex poetry waiting to be mined; but there are hundreds of people whose lives he touched as professor, lecturer, and friend who are ready to testify now as to the impact he made on them. Although Tolson seldom broached the subject of death in those last days in August, 1966, he undoubtedly pondered, as he considered his work and his life, the lines he had penned some twenty years before in South Texas:

> I harbor
> One fear
> If death
> Crouch near.
> Does my
> Creed span
> The Gulf
> Of Man?
>
> And when
> I go
> In calm
> Or blow
> From mice
> And men,
> Selah!
> What . . . then? [35]

Notes and References

Chapter One

1. All quotations and descriptions of Tolson's reactions to various incidents are the result of notes taken during conversations with him or during lectures he gave, unless otherwise indicated.

2. Conversation with Mrs. Helen Tolson Wilson in Hampton, Virginia, August, 1967.

3. Notebook is with Tolson's unpublished papers collected by Mrs. Ruth Tolson, Washington, D.C.

4. Melvin B. Tolson, "A Poet's Odyssey," *Anger, and Beyond,* ed. Herbert Hill (New York, 1966), p. 193.

5. Tolson, "A Poet's Odyssey," pp. 193–94.

6. Taped conversation with Professor and Mrs. M. B. Tolson, August, 1965.

7. Conversation with M. B. Tolson, Jr., October, 1966.

8. Dudley Randall, "Portrait of a Poet as Raconteur," *Negro Digest,* XV, 3 (January, 1966), 57.

9. Tolson's unpublished notes collected by Mrs. Ruth Tolson, Washington, D.C.

10. Randall, "Portrait of a Poet as Raconteur," p. 56.

11. Maxwell Perkins, letter to M. B. Tolson, November 28, 1939; Tolson's unpublished papers collected by Mrs. Ruth Tolson, Washington, D.C.

12. A recent anthology of black literature was named for the poem: *Dark Symphony,* ed. James A. Emmanuel and Theodore L. Gross (New York, 1968).

13. Melvin B. Tolson, *Rendezvous with America* (New York, 1944), p. 25.

14. Conversation with M. B. Tolson, Jr., October, 1966.

15. Ramona Lowe, "Poem 'Rendezvous with America' Wins Fame for Melvin Tolson," Chicago *Defender,* New York Bureau, February 24, 1945.

16. Conversation with M. B. Tolson, Jr., October, 1966.

17. William Rose Benét, "Two Powerful Negro Poets," *Saturday Review* (March 24, 1945), p. 35.

18. Melvin B. Tolson, lecture for poetry workshop, Central State University, Edmond, Oklahoma, June, 1965.

19. A copy of this article is with the Tolson papers collected by Mrs. Ruth Tolson, Washington, D.C.

20. Lorenzo D. Turner, "Words for a Vast Music," *Poetry*, LXXXVI (June, 1955), 174–76.

21. John Ciardi, letter to Richard L. Brown, assistant director, Bread Loaf Writers' Conference, February 27, 1954; carbon copy among Tolson's unpublished papers collected by Mrs. Ruth Tolson, Washington, D.C.

22. Melvin B. Tolson, "Caviar and Cabbages," Washington *Tribune*, February 9, 1939.

23. Star of Africa conferred on Tolson, May 6, 1954.

24. Margaret Williams Wade, English major who was enrolled in Tolson's English literature class in 1964–65.

25. Conversation with Juanita Goff, former student of Tolson at Langston University; also, classroom lectures, spring, 1965.

26. Printed in Obsequies of Melvin B. Tolson, September 3, 1966; among Tolson's papers collected by Mrs. Ruth Tolson, Washington, D.C.

27. Classroom lecture, Langston University, March, 1965.

28. Conversation with M. B. Tolson, Jr., January, 1967.

29. This review also appears as the Introduction to *Harlem Gallery: Book I, The Curator* (New York, 1965).

30. David Llorens, "Seeking a New Image: Writers Converge at Fisk University," *Negro Digest*, XV, 8 (June, 1966), 60, 62–63.

Chapter Two

1. See Melvin B. Tolson, "The Tragedy of the Yarr Karr," *The Wild Cat*, Wiley College (Marshall, Texas, 1926), pp. 193–98.

2. Melvin B. Tolson, unpublished notes collected by Mrs. Ruth Tolson, Washington, D.C.

3. Margaret Walker, *New Adventures into Poetry* (n.d.). Quotation among Tolson's unpublished notes collected by Mrs. Ruth Tolson, Washington, D.C.

4. Nathaniel Tillman, "The Poet Speaks," *Phylon*, 4 (Winter, 1944), 391.

5. Melvin B. Tolson, Arts and Sciences Banquet, Oklahoma State University, Stillwater, Oklahoma, February, 1966.

6. Robert Hillyer, "Among the New Volumes of Verse," New York *Times*, December 10, 1944, p. 29.

7. J. K., "Unprejudiced Poems," Raleigh (North Carolina) *Observer*, October 8, 1944.

8. William Rose Benét, "Two Powerful Negro Poets," p. 35.

9. Review (anon.), Los Angeles *Times* (n.d.). Quoted in "Wiley English Professor Writes Best Seller," Wiley (Marshall, Texas) *Reporter*, May, 1945. Clipping among Tolson's unpublished notes collected by Mrs. Ruth Tolson, Washington, D.C.

10. Melvin B. Tolson, "Caviar and Cabbages," November 26, 1938.

11. Ramona Lowe, "Poem 'Rendezvous with America' Wins Fame for Melvin Tolson," Chicago *Defender*, February 24, 1945.

12. Melvin B. Tolson, lecture, Oklahoma Poetry Society, Oklahoma City Art Center, July 25, 1965.

13. Melvin B. Tolson, Cut #C, p. 1. Manuscript for tape made for University of Wisconsin Educational Radio Station; taped at University of Oklahoma, Norman, Oklahoma, March 8, 1965.

14. Nathaniel Tillman, "The Poet Speaks," p. 390.

15. Arthur E. Burke, "Book Review: Lyrico-Dramatic," *The Crisis* (January, 1945), p. 61.

16. Margaret Walker, *New Adventures into Poetry* (n.d.). Quotation among Tolson's unpublished notes collected by Mrs. Ruth Tolson, Washington, D.C.

17. Tolson's unpublished notes collected by Mrs. Ruth Tolson, Washington, D.C.

18. Nathaniel Tillman, "The Poet Speaks," p. 389.

19. P. L. Prattis (n.d.). Quotation among Tolson's unpublished notes collected by Mrs. Ruth Tolson, Washington, D.C.

20. Richard Wright (n.d.). Clipping among Tolson's unpublished notes collected by Mrs. Ruth Tolson, Washington, D.C.

21. James Farmer, *Equality* (n.d.). Quotation among Tolson's unpublished notes collected by Mrs. Ruth Tolson, Washington, D.C.

22. Margaret Walker, *New Adventures into Poetry* (n.d.). Quotation among Tolson's unpublished notes collected by Mrs. Ruth Tolson, Washington, D.C.

23. Robert Hillyer, "Among the New Volumes of Verse," p. 29.

24. William Rose Benét, "Two Powerful Negro Poets," p. 35.

25. Richard Ellmann, *Eminent Domain* (New York, 1967), p. 35.

26. Eliot won the Nobel Prize in 1948, so it is the author's assumption that these comments were written between 1948 and 1950.

Chapter Three

1. Letter from George Dillon to M. B. Tolson, September 27, 1948; Tolson's unpublished papers collected by Ruth Tolson, Washington, D.C.

2. Ransom, Tate, Davidson, Warren, Merrill Moore, Laura Riding, Jesse Wills, Alec B. Stevenson, Walter Clyde Curry, Stanley Johnson,

Sidney M. Hirsch, James Frank, William Y. Elliott, William Frierson, Ridley Wills, and Alfred Starr.

3. Louise Cowan, Introduction, *The Fugitive Group* (Baton Rouge, Louisiana, 1968), p. xxiii.

4. Dudley Randall, "Portrait of a Poet as Raconteur," p. 56.

5. Allen Tate, Preface, *Libretto for the Republic of Liberia* (New York, 1953), p. [i].

6. *Ibid.*, p. [iii].

7. Karl Shapiro, author of the Introduction to *Harlem Gallery*, attacks Tate's "reasons" for accepting *Libretto* and claims that Tolson's last two books are "the Negro satire upon the poetic tradition of the Eliots and Tates." See Karl Shapiro, "Decolonization of American Literature," *Wilson Library Bulletin* (June, 1965), pp. 843–54.

8. *Harlem Gallery* (New York, 1965), p. 54.

9. "An Evening With M. B. Tolson," lecture, Fine Arts Week, I. W. Young Auditorium, Langston University, Langston, Oklahoma, April 8, 1965.

10. Dan McCall, "The Quicksilver Sparrow of M. B. Tolson," *American Quarterly*, XVIII, 3 (Fall, 1966), 539.

11. Allen Tate, Preface, *Libretto*, p. [i].

12. Charles Morrow Wilson, *Liberia* (New York, 1947), pp. 7–95.

13. McCall, "The Quicksilver Sparrow of M. B. Tolson," p. 538.

14. Stéphane Mallarmé, "Art for All," 1862, *Prose Poems, Essays, and Letters*, tr. Bradford Cook (Baltimore, 1965), p. 13; reprinted in "Art as Aristocratic Mystery," *The Modern Tradition*, eds. Richard Ellmann and Charles Feidelson, Jr. (New York, 1965), p. 208.

15. Tolson's unpublished notes collected by Mrs. Ruth Tolson, Washington, D.C.

16. Arthur Rimbaud, letters to George Izambard and Paul Demeny, 1871. *Selected Verses*, ed. and tr. Oliver Bernard, 1962, pp. 5–16; in "The Poet as Revolutionary Seer," *The Modern Tradition*, eds. Richard Ellmann and Charles Feidelson, Jr. (New York, 1965), p. 204.

17. Karl Shapiro, "Decolonization of American Literature," *Wilson Library Bulletin* (June, 1965), p. 853.

18. Melvin B. Tolson, "A Poet's Odyssey," p. 195.

19. Clay was called the "Great Pacificator" because of his ability to reconcile differences of opinion.

20. "Charles Turner Torrey," *Encyclopedia Americana* (New York, 1953), XXVI, 710.

21. Selden Rodman, "On Vistas Undreamt," New York *Times Book Review*, LIX, 4, January 24, 1954, p. 10.

22. Melvin B. Tolson, "A Poet's Odyssey," p. 185.

23. Interview, M. B. Tolson, Jr., September, 1968.

24. Stanley Hyman, *The Tangled Bush* (New York, 1962), p. 347.

25. John Ciardi, "Recent Verse," *Nation,* CLXXVIII (February 27, 1954), p. 183.

26. According to Tolson's notes at the end of the book, the code words for the A-bombs. The message indicating success in developing the A-bomb read: "Baby boy born today mother and child doing well."

27. Professor Pangloss in Voltaire's *Candide* taught metaphysico-theologo-cosmolonigology in proving that there is no effect without a cause in this best of all possible worlds (Ch. I, p. 2).

28. Allen Tate, Preface, *Libretto,* p. [ii].

29. McCall, "The Quicksilver Sparrow of M. B. Tolson," p. 542.

30. Selden Rodman, "On Vistas Undreamt," p. 10.

31. James Tulip, "Afro-American Poet—M. B. Tolson," *Poetry, Australia,* 10 (June, 1966).

32. Letter of Melvin B. Tolson is dated January 26, 1954. Whether or not the finished copy was ever mailed is not known.

33. John Ciardi, "Recent Verse," p. 183.

34. Letter from Jacob Steinberg, Managing Editor, Twayne Publishers, Inc., September 21, 1953, to M. B. Tolson; among Tolson's papers collected by Mrs. Ruth Tolson, Washington, D.C.

35. Howard Fussiner, "A Mature Voice Speaks," *Phylon,* XV, 1 (1st quarter, 1954), 96–97.

36. Allen Tate, Preface, *Libretto,* p. [ii].

37. John Ciardi, "Recent Verse," p. 183.

38. Karl Shapiro, Introduction, *Harlem Gallery,* p. 14.

Chapter Four

1. Jack Bickham, "Langston Poet May Signal New Era," *The Sunday Oklahoman,* May 23, 1965, p. 10.

2. Melvin B. Tolson, Cut B, manuscript of tape made for University of Wisconsin educational radio station, March 10, 1965.

3. "Key Words," p. 3; Tolson's unpublished notes collected by Mrs. Ruth Tolson, Washington, D.C.

4. Virginia Scott Miner, "A 'Great Poet' Unknown in Our Own Mid-West," The Kansas City *Star,* July 25, 1965.

5. James Tulip, "Afro-American Poet—M. B. Tolson," *Poetry* (Australia), n.p.

6. Laurence Lieberman, "Poetry Chronicle," *The Hudson Review* (Autumn, 1965), p. 457.

7. Robert Donald Spector, "The Poet's Voice in the Crowd," *Saturday Review* (August 7, 1965), p. 29.

8. *"Melvin B. Tolson:* An Interview," *Anger, and Beyond,* ed. Herbert Hill (New York, 1966), pp. 194–95. The interview was conducted by Mrs. Moxye W. King, at that time chairman of the Department of

English and Modern Languages, Langston University, Langston, Oklahoma (March 10, 1965).

9. Lieberman, "Poetry Chronicle," p. 456.

10. Karl Shapiro, Introduction, *Harlem Gallery*, p. 14.

11. Tolson, Cut B, manuscript of tape made for University of Wisconsin educational radio station, March 10, 1965.

12. " 'Lord of the flies' is a translation of the Hebrew *Ba'alzevuv* (Beelzebub in Greek). It has been suggested that it was a mistranslation of a mistransliterated word which gave us this pungent and suggestive name for the Devil, a devil whose name suggests that he is devoted to decay, destruction, demoralization, hysteria, and panic. . . ." See William Golding, "Notes," *Lord of the Flies* (New York, 1959), p. 190.

13. E. Franklin Frazier, *Black Bourgeoisie* (Glencoe, Illinois, 1957), p. 26.

14. *Ibid.*, p. 25.

15. *Ibid.*, p. 206.

16. Melvin B. Tolson, "Key Words," p. 3; Tolson's unpublished notes collected by Mrs. Ruth Tolson, Washington, D.C.

17. "The Ballad of John Henry" appears in *Dark Symphony*, eds. James A. Emmanuel and Theodore L. Gross (New York, 1968), pp. 473–76.

18. *"Melvin B. Tolson:* An Interview," pp. 194–95.

19. Toothed wheel which rolls upon another toothed wheel.

20. M. B. Tolson, unpublished notes collected by Mrs. Ruth Tolson, Washington, D.C.

21. Virginia Scott Miner, "A 'Great Poet' Unknown in Our Own Mid-West," Kansas City *Star.*

22. Laurence Lieberman, "Poetry Chronicle," p. 456.

23. Sarah Webster Fabio, "Who Speaks Negro?," *Negro Digest,* XVI, 2 (December, 1966), 54.

24. Karl Shapiro, "Decolonization of American Literature," p. 852.

25. Josephine Jacobsen, "Books in Review," [Baltimore, Md.] *Evening Sun,* November 2, 1965, p. A–20; Virginia Scott Miner, "A 'Great Poet' Unknown in Our Own Mid-West"; Robert Donald Spector, "The Poet's Voice in the Crowd," p. 29.

26. Laurence Lieberman, "Poetry Chronicle," p. 457.

27. James Tulip, "Afro-American Poet—M. B. Tolson," *Poetry,* Australia, n.p.

28. David Littlejohn, "Negro Writers Today: The Poets," *Black on White: A Critical Survey of Writing by American Negroes* (New York, 1966), p. 82.

29. "A New Light on the Invisible," (anon. rev.), *Literary Supplement,* London *Times,* November 25, 1965, p. 1049.

30. David Daiches, *Literary Essays* (1956); reprinted in "Religion, Poetry, and the 'Dilemma' of the Modern Writer," *Perspectives in Contemporary Criticism,* ed. Sheldon N. Grebstein (New York, 1968), p. 57.

31. Robert Donald Spector, "The Poet's Voice in the Crowd," p. 29.

32. "A New Light on the Invisible," (anon. rev.), p. 1049.

Chapter Five

1. Karl Shapiro, Introduction, *Harlem Gallery,* p. 11.

2. M. B. Tolson, draft of a letter to Ben and Kate Bell, December 28, 1961; Tolson's unpublished papers collected by Mrs. Ruth Tolson, Washington, D.C.

3. Don Lee, "On *Kaleidoscope* and Robert Hayden," *Negro Digest,* 3 (January, 1968), p. 91.

4. David Llorens, "Black Don Lee," *Ebony,* XXIV, 5 (March, 1969), 74.

5. Effie Lee Newsome, "Melvin B. Tolson, *Rendezvous with America,*" *The Negro College Quarterly,* II, 4 (December, 1949), 171–72.

6. Don Lee, "On *Kaleidoscope* and Robert Hayden," p. 90.

7. Paul Breman, "Poetry into the Sixties," *Poetry and Drama; The Black American Writer,* Vol. II, ed. C. W. E. Bigsby (Baltimore, 1969), p. 101.

8. Sarah Webster Fabio, "Who Speaks Negro?," p. 54.

9. Don Lee, "On *Kaleidoscope* and Robert Hayden," p. 90.

10. Clinton Oliver, seminar on "Definitive Qualities of Black Literature," Oklahoma State University, Stillwater, Oklahoma, February 13, 1969.

11. "A Survey: Black Writers' Views on Literary Lions and Values," *Negro Digest,* XVII, 3 (January, 1968), 12.

12. *Ibid.,* p. 13.

13. Arna Bontemps, conversation, Negro History Week, Langston University, Langston, Oklahoma, February 12, 1969.

14. Abraham Chapman, ed., *Black Voices* (New York, 1968), p. 40.

15. Gwendolyn Brooks, Seminar on Black Poetry, Negro History Week, Langston University, Langston, Oklahoma, February 10, 1969.

16. James Emmanuel and Theodore Gross, eds., *Dark Symphony,* p. 472.

17. Dolphin G. Thompson, "Tolson's Gallery Brings Poetry Home," *The Negro History Bulletin,* XXIX, 3 (December, 1965), 69.

18. J. A. Ramsaran, "The 'Twice-Born' Artists' Silent Revolution," *Black World* (May, 1971), pp. 60, 61.

19. M. B. Tolson, "The Contributors' Column," *Atlantic Monthly* (September, 1941), p. v.

20. M. B. Tolson, Jr., Conversation, March, 1969.

21. Jack Bickham, "A Superbly Successful Human Being," the Oklahoma *Courier*, September 9, 1966, p. 5.

22. Emmanuel and Gross, eds., *Dark Symphony*, p. 472.

23. Karl Shapiro, Introduction, *Harlem Gallery*, p. 14.

24. Chappell White, "Anderson 'Variations' Shows Writer's Skill," the Atlantic *Journal*, May 27, 1970.

25. Bob Rohrer, "Anderson Premiere Haunting," the *Atlantic Constitution*, May 27, 1970.

26. M. B. Tolson, Jr., lecture for humanities class, Langston University, Langston, Oklahoma, April, 1970.

27. T. S. Eliot, "The Music of Poetry," *Partisan Review*, IX, No. 6 (November–December, 1942), 461–62.

28. C. K. Stead, *The New Poetic* (London, 1964), p. 29.

29. Karl Shapiro, *A Primer for Poets* (Lincoln, Nebraska, 1953), p. 41.

30. Herbert Hill, "In Memory of M. B. Tolson . . . 1900–1966," *Tuesday* (November, 1966), p. 26.

31. M. B. Tolson, Jr., lecture for humanities class, Langston University, Langston, Oklahoma, April, 1970.

32. M. B. Tolson, conversation with Dr. Walter L. Jones, dean of academic affairs, Langston University, Langston, Oklahoma, June, 1966.

33. Jack Bickham, "A Superbly Successful Human Being," p. 5.

34. Robert Donald Spector, "A Poet's Voice in the Crowd," p. 29.

35. M. B. Tolson, "Song for Myself," *Rendezvous with America*, pp. 50–51.

Selected Bibliography

PRIMARY SOURCES

1. Published Works

"Abraham Lincoln of Rock Spring Farms," *Soon, One Morning: New Writing by American Negroes.* Ed. Herbert Hill. New York: Alfred A. Knopf, 1963.

"African China," "Phi" (*Harlem Gallery*), *Kaleidoscope.* Ed. Robert Hayden. New York: Harcourt, Brace, and World, Inc., 1967.

"Alpha," "Beta," "Gamma," "Delta," "Epsilon," "Zeta," "Eta," *Prairie Schooner*, XXXV, 3 (Fall, 1961), 243–64.

"The Braggart" (*Rendezvous with America*), *Common Ground*, IV, 4 (Summer, 1944), 74.

"Dr. Harvey Whyte," *Modern Monthly* (August, 1937), p. 10.

"An Ex-Judge at the Bar," "Dark Symphony" (*Rendezvous with America*); "Psi" (*Harlem Gallery*), *Black Voices.* Ed. Abraham Chapman. New York: The New American Library, 1968.

"The Ballad of the Rattlesnake" (*Rendezvous with America*), *An Introduction to Literature.* Eds. Mary Rohrberger, Samuel H. Woods, Jr., and Bernard F. Dukore. New York: Random House, 1968.

"Caviar and Cabbages," Washington *Tribune*, November 26, 1938, and February 9, 1939.

"Claude McKay's Art," *Poetry*, XXCIII (February, 1954), 287–90.

"The Contributors' Column," *Atlantic Monthly*, CLXVIII, 3 (September, 1941), v.

Cuts A, B, C, and D. Manuscript for tape made for distribution from University of Wisconsin Education Radio Station; taped March 8, 1965. Reprinted as "A Poet's Odyssey" in *Anger, and Beyond.* Ed. Herbert Hill. New York: Harper and Row, 1966.

"Dark Symphony," *Atlantic Monthly*, CLXVIII, 3 (September, 1941), 314–17.

"Dark Symphony," *Auch Ich Bin Amerika.* Ed. Stephan Hermlin, n.d.

Information among Tolson's unpublished notes collected by Mrs. Ruth Tolson, Washington, D.C.

"Dark Symphony" (*Rendezvous with America*), *The Black Experience*. Ed. Francis E. Kearns. New York: The Viking Press, 1970.

"Dark Symphony" (*Rendezvous with America*); "Lambda" (*Harlem Gallery*); "Do" (*Libretto for the Republic of Liberia*), *The Poetry of the Negro, 1764–1970; An Anthology*, rev. ed. Eds. Langston Hughes and Arna Bontemps. Garden City, New York: Doubleday, 1970.

"Dr. Harvey Whyte," *Modern Monthly* (August, 1937), p. 10.

"E. & O. E.," *Poetry*, LXXVIII, 7 (September, 1951), 330–42, 369–372.

"Goodbye Christ," Pittsburgh *Courier*, XXIII, January 26, 1933, pp. 10–11.

"Hamuel Gutterman," *Modern Monthly* (April, 1937), p. 7.

"Jacob Nollen," *Modern Monthly* (May, 1937), p. 10.

"Kikes, Bohunks, Crackers, Dagos, Niggers," *The Modern Quarterly*, XI, 4 (Autumn, 1939), 18–19.

"From *Libretto for the Republic of Liberia*," *Poetry*, LXXVI, 4 (July, 1950), 208–15.

"From 'Xi' " (*Harlem Gallery*), *Dark Symphony*. Eds. James Emmanuel and Theodore L. Gross. New York: The Free Press, 1968.

Harlem Gallery: Book I, The Curator. New York: Twayne Publishers, 1965.

"The Man from Halicarnassus," *Poetry*, LXXXI, 1 (October, 1952), 75–77.

Libretto for the Republic of Liberia. New York: Twayne Publishers, 1953.

"Miles to Go with Black Ulysses," *Book Week*, New York *Herald Tribune*, III, 24 (February 20, 1966), 2, 12.

"Rendezvous with America," *Common Ground* (Summer, 1942), pp. 3–9.

Rendezvous with America. New York: Dodd, Mead and Company, 1944.

"Richard Wright: *Native Son*," *The Modern Quarterly*, XI, 5 (Winter, 1939), 19–24.

"A Song for Myself" (*Rendezvous with America*), *Phylon*, IV, 4 (1945), 351–52.

"The Tragedy of the Yarr Karr," *The* (Wiley College) *Wild Cat* (1926), pp. 193–98.

"Uncle Walt," *The Modern Quarterly*, X, 7 (March, 1938), 10.

"Vergil Ragsdale," *The Modern Quarterly*, XI, 2 (Winter, 1939), 48.

"*Woodcuts for America*: 'Old Man Michael,' 'The Gallows,' 'The Man

Inside,' 'When Great Dogs Fight,'" *Common Ground* (Spring, 1943), pp. 38–43.

"Xi" (*Harlem Gallery*), *3000 Years of Black Poetry; An Anthology.* Eds. Alan Lomax and Raoul Abdul. New York: Dodd, Mead and Company, 1970.

2. Unpublished Works

"An Evening with M. B. Tolson," lecture, Fine Arts Week, Langston University, Langston, Oklahoma, April 8, 1965; notes of Joy Flasch, Coyle, Oklahoma.

Classroom lectures of Melvin B. Tolson, Langston University, Langston, Oklahoma, 1964–1966; notes of Joy Flasch, Coyle, Oklahoma.

Conversations with Melvin B. Tolson, Langston, Oklahoma, 1964–66; notes of Joy Flasch, Coyle, Oklahoma.

"Key Words" in *Harlem Gallery;* Tolson's papers collected by Mrs. Ruth Tolson, Washington, D.C.

"The Ladder of the Mind," address at Arts and Sciences Banquet, Oklahoma State University, Stillwater, Oklahoma, February 15, 1966; notes of Joy Flasch, Coyle, Oklahoma.

Lecture for Oklahoma Poetry Society, Oklahoma City Art Center, Oklahoma City, Oklahoma, July 25, 1965; notes of Joy Flasch, Coyle, Oklahoma.

Lecture for Poetry Workshop, Central State University, Edmond, Oklahoma, June, 1965; notes of Joy Flasch, Coyle, Oklahoma.

Letters, notebooks, and papers of Melvin B. Tolson; collected by Mrs. Ruth Tolson, Washington, D.C.

Tape of conversation with Professor and Mrs. M. B. Tolson, August, 1965; tape made by Joy Flasch, Coyle, Oklahoma.

SECONDARY SOURCES

1. Books

BIGSBY, C. W. E. "The Black American Writer." *The Black American Writer: Fiction,* I. Baltimore: Penguin Books, Inc., 1969. In-depth analysis of black literature of worth in twentieth century and of the dilemma of the black American writer.

BREMAN, PAUL. "Poetry into the Sixties." *The Black American Writer: Poetry and Drama,* II. Ed. C. W. E. Bigsby. Baltimore: Penguin Books, Inc., 1969. Celebrates emergence of black poetry and Black Esthetic in recent years.

CHAPMAN, ABRAHAM, ed. *Black Voices*. New York: The New American Library, 1968. Preface of anthology comments on development of black writers in America.

COWAN, LOUISE. *The Fugitive Group*. Baton Rouge, Louisiana: Louisiana State University Press, 1968. Describes influence of Southern Agrarian poets on one another during period in which Tolson resided in same city. Defines influence of Fugitive poets on one another and on twentieth-century poetry.

DAICHES, DAVID. *Literary Essays* (1956). Reprinted in "Religion, Poetry, and the 'Dilemma' of the Modern Writer," *Perspectives in Contemporary Criticism*. Ed. Sheldon N. Grebstein. New York: Harper and Row, 1968. Presents Daiches' theory concerning limitations of Eliot's influence on other poets.

DOYLE, JOHN R. *The Poetry of Robert Frost*. New York: Hafner Publishing Company, Inc., 1962. Describes Frost's development as poet.

ELLMANN, RICHARD. *Eminent Domain*. New York: Oxford University Press, 1967. Describes influence of Irish, British, and American poets on one another around turn of twentieth century.

ELLMANN, RICHARD and CHARLES FEIDELSON, JR., eds. *The Modern Tradition*. New York: Oxford University Press, 1965. Anthology contains excerpts from past century of literary criticism.

EMMANUEL, JAMES A. *Langston Hughes*. New York: Twayne Publishers, 1967. Critical biography which describes Hughes's development as black writer in twentieth century.

EMMANUEL, JAMES, and THEODORE L. GROSS, eds. *Dark Symphony*. New York: The Free Press, 1968. Anthology of black literature. Editors comment on Tolson as black poet.

FRAZIER, E. FRANKLIN. *Black Bourgeoisie*. Glencoe, Illinois: Falcon's Wing Press, 1957. Sociological work analyzing segment of Afro-American population. Tolson makes several allusions to this work in *Harlem Gallery*.

FRYE, NORTHRUP. *T. S. Eliot*. New York: Grove Press, Inc., 1963. Analysis of Eliot's life and work, giving details of his development as major twentieth-century poet.

FUSSELL, PAUL, JR. *Poetic Meter and Poetic Form*. New York: Random House, 1968. Analysis of types of poetic meter and form. Describes effect secured by usage of each.

GOLDING, WILLIAM. "Notes." *Lord of the Flies*. New York: Capricorn Books, 1959. Information in Notes explains allusion in line five of "Alpha" in *Harlem Gallery*.

HEADINGS, PHILLIP. *T. S. Eliot*. New York: Twayne Publishers, Inc., 1964. Biographical and critical work follows Eliot's development as major twentieth-century poet.

HYMAN, STANLEY. *The Tangled Bank*. New York: Atheneum, 1962. In chapter on "gallows-humor" of oppressed peoples, Hyman alludes to line 294 in "Ti" in *Libretto*.

LITTLEJOHN, DAVID. *Black on White: A Critical Survey of Writing by American Negroes*. New York: Grossman Publishers, 1966. Anthology contains critical commentary on black American writers.

MALLARMÉ, STÉPHANE. "Art for All" (1862). *Prose Poems, Essays, and Letters*. Tr. Bradford Cook (Baltimore, 1956). Reprinted in "Art as Aristocratic Mystery." *The Modern Tradition*. Eds. Richard Ellmann and Charles Feidelson, Jr. New York: Oxford University Press, 1965. Excerpt contains admonition to poets not to "write down" to masses.

NELSON, JOHN H. and OSCAR CARGILL. *Contemporary Trends: American Literature Since 1900*. New York: The Macmillan Company, 1949. Traces development of American literature and literary criticism in twentieth century.

RIMBAUD, ARTHUR. Letters to George Izambard and Paul Demeny (1871) *Selected Verses*. Ed. and trans. Oliver Bernard (1962). Reprinted in "The Poet as Revolutionary Seer," *The Modern Tradition*. Eds. Richard Ellmann and Charles Feidelson, Jr. New York: Oxford University Press, 1965. Contains quotation about poet as prophet, which can be applied to Tolson, particularly in final sections of *Libretto*.

SCOTT, WILBUR, ed. *Five Approaches of Literary Criticism*. New York: The Macmillan Company, 1968. Analysis of five modern modes of criticism applicable to literature. Gives specific examples showing application of approaches to literary works.

SHAPIRO, KARL. Introduction. *Harlem Gallery: Book I, The Curator*. New York: Twayne Publishers, Inc., 1965. Introduction appeared in New York *Herald Tribune*, January 10, 1965, as prepublication review of *Harlem Gallery*.

————. *A Primer for Poets*. Lincoln, Nebraska: University of Nebraska Press, 1953. Analyzes process of writing poetry; suggests effects of certain poetic devices.

STEAD, C. K. *The New Poetic*. London: Hutchinson University Library, 1964. Analysis of development of "New Poetry" of Yeats, Eliot, and their contemporaries.

TATE, ALLEN. Preface. *Libretto for the Republic of Liberia*. New York: Twayne Publishers, Inc., 1953. Introduction to *Libretto* names Tolson as one of the outstanding twentieth-century black poets.

THOMPSON, LAWRANCE. *Robert Frost, The Early Years, 1874–1915*. New York: Holt, Rinehart, and Winston, 1966. Critical biography of Frost's early years; traces his development as a poet.

WELLEK, RENÉ. *Concepts of Criticism.* New Haven: Yale University Press, 1964. Series of essays concerns methods of studying literary works. Defines ideal goals to be achieved by new methods of criticism and analyzes reviews of works done by other scholars to show wherein methods have succeeded and failed.

WILSON, CHARLES M. *Liberia.* New York: W. Sloane Associates, 1947. History of founding and development of Liberia as a republic.

WINTERS, YVOR. "The Significance of *The Bridge* by Hart Crane," *In Defense of Reason.* Denver: Alan Swallow, 1947. Analysis of work which influenced Tolson's concept of form and climax.

2. Articles and Reviews

BENÉT, WILLIAM. "Two Powerful Negro Poets," *Saturday Review* (March 24, 1945), pp. 35–6. Review of *Rendezvous with America.*

BICKMAN, JACK. "Flowers of Hope," Orbit, *Sunday Oklahoman,* August 29, 1965, pp. 6–9. Feature article on Tolson as Oklahoma poet to whom long overdue recognition had at last come.

————. "Langston Poet May Signal New Era," *Sunday Oklahoman,* May 23, 1965, p. 10. Feature article hailing, *Harlem Gallery.*

————. "A Superbly Successful Human Being," Oklahoma *Courier,* September 9, 1966, p. 5. Personal tribute and memorial to Tolson.

"Books in Brief: *Rendezvous with America.*" Anon. rev., *The Christian Century,* LXI (September 20, 1944), 1078–79, Review of *Rendezvous with America.*

BURKE, ARTHUR. "Book Review: Lyrico-Dramatic," *The Crisis* (January, 1945), p. 61. Review of *Rendezvous with America.*

CIARDI, JOHN. "Recent Verse," *The Nation* (February 27, 1954), p. 183. Review of *Libretto.*

DELANCEY, ROSE MARY. "Tolson Hailed as Great Poet," Fort Wayne *News-Sentinel,* April 24, 1965, p. 4–A. Review of *Harlem Gallery.*

ELIOT, T. S. "The Music of Poetry," *Partisan Review,* IX, 6 (November-December, 1942), 450–64. Eliot discusses several of his objectives as poet.

————. "A Talk on Dante," *Kenyon Review,* XIV (Spring, 1952), 179–80. Eliot traces some of the sources which exerted influence on him as a poet.

"The Evils of Too Much Print." Anon. rev., *Literary Digest,* XLII (March 11, 1911), 461. Article notes Yeats's emphasis on "the voice" as vehicle for communication in poetry and drama.

FABIO, SARAH WEBSTER. "Who Speaks Negro?," *Negro Digest*, XVI, 2 (December, 1966), 54–58. Author challenges Karl Shapiro's statement that Tolson writes "in Negro."

FARMER, JAMES. *Equality*, n.d. Comments about Tolson as a black poet. Information in Tolson's unpublished papers collected by Mrs. Ruth Tolson, Washington, D.C.

FLASCH, JOY. "Greatness Defined," Letters to the Book Review Editor, *Saturday Review* (September 5, 1965), p. 39. Letter from colleague of M. B. Tolson gives insight into Tolson the man.

————. "Humor and Satire in the Poetry of M. B. Tolson," *Satire Newsletter*, VII, 1 (Fall, 1969), 29–36. Analysis of humor and satire in Tolson's poetry, with emphasis on *Harlem Gallery*.

————. "M. B. Tolson, A Great American Poet," *Oklahoma Librarian*, XVIII, 4 (October, 1968), 116–18. Introduction to Tolson's life and work.

FUSSINER, HOWARD R. "A Mature Voice Speaks," *Phylon*, XV, 1 (1st quarter, 1954), 96–97. Review of *Libretto*.

HILL, HERBERT. "In Memory of M. B. Tolson . . . 1900–1966," *Tuesday* (November, 1966), p. 26. Tribute to Tolson by friend and literary critic.

HILLYER, ROBERT. "Among the New Volumes of Verse," New York *Times*, December 10, 1944, p. 29. Review of *Rendezvous with America*.

HUGHES, LANGSTON. "Here to Yonder," Chicago *Defender*, December 15, 1945. Comment about *Rendezvous with America*.

JACOBSEN, JOSEPHINE. "Books in Review," (Baltimore, Maryland) *Evening Sun*, November 2, 1965, p. A–20. Review of *Harlem Gallery*.

K., J. "Unprejudiced Poems," Raleigh (North Carolina) *Observer*, October 8, 1944. Review of *Rendezvous with America*.

"Langston Hears Poet's 'Odyssey,'" *Daily Oklahoman*, April 9, 1965, p. 16. Review of Tolson's address at Langston University (Langston, Oklahoma) Fine Arts Festival.

"Lauded Oklahoma Poet Working Hard After Battle With Cancer," *Daily Oklahoman*, February 4, 1965, p. 11. Human interest story on Tolson as long-unrecognized poet exhibiting courage in struggle with cancer.

"Laureate Poet Explains Principles at Banquet," the [Oklahoma State University] *Daily O'Collegian*, LXXI, 90, February 16, p. 1. Review of address given by Tolson at Oklahoma State University (Stillwater, Oklahoma) Arts and Sciences banquet.

LEE, DON L. "On *Kaleidoscope* and Robert Hayden," *Negro Digest*, XVII, 3 (January, 1968), 51–52, 90–94. Review of black anthology contains brief criticism of Tolson as black poet.

"Let's Erect a Monument," Wiley (Marshall, Texas) *Reporter,* August 23, 1948. Tribute to Tolson as professor, poet, debate and drama coach, and philosopher.

"Liberia Honors Poet Laureate from Oklahoma," *Daily Oklahoman,* November 24, 1965, p. 10. News story about reception given in Liberian Embassy, Washington, D.C., in honor of Tolson.

LIEBERMAN, LAURENCE, "Poetry Chronicle," *The Hudson Review* (Autumn, 1965), pp. 455–60. Review of *Harlem Gallery.*

LLORENS, DAVID. "Black Don Lee," *Ebony,* XXIV, 5 (March, 1969), 72–80. Article contains excerpt from Tolson's poem "The Poet" (*Rendezvous with America*) which Llorens uses to describe Lee.

————. "Seeking a New Image: Writers Converge at Fisk University," *Negro Digest,* XV, 8 (June, 1966), 54–68. Feature story on one of Tolson's final public appearances.

LOWE, RAMONA. "Poem 'Rendezvous with America' Wins Fame for Melvin Tolson," Chicago *Defender,* New York Bureau, February 24, 1945. Review of *Rendezvous with America.*

M., S. "The Death of Simple," *Newsweek* (June 5, 1967), p. 104. Tribute to Langston Hughes and his best-known character.

McCALL, DAN. "The Quicksilver Sparrow of M. B. Tolson," *American Quarterly,* XVIII, 3 (Fall, 1966), 538–42. Analysis of passage from *Libretto* and evaluation of the ode.

MINER, VIRGINIA SCOTT, "A 'Great Poet' Unknown in Our Own Midwest," the Kansas City *Star,* July 25, 1965. Review of *Harlem Gallery.*

MONTGOMERY, Ed. "Ten State Authors Win Library Week Salute," *Sunday Oklahoman,* April 16, 1967, p. 23. Tribute to Tolson as an outstanding Oklahoma poet.

"A New Light on the Invisible," Anon. rev., the (London) *Times Literary Supplement,* November 25, 1965, p. 1049. Review of *Harlem Gallery.*

NEWSOME, EFFIE LEE. "Melvin B. Tolson, *Rendezvous with America,*" *Negro College Quarterly,* II, 4 (December, 1944), 171–72. Review of *Rendezvous with America.*

PRATTIS, P. L. Pittsburgh *Courier,* n.d. Review of *Rendezvous with America.* Information among Tolson's unpublished papers collected by Ruth Tolson, Washington, D.C.

RAMSARAN, J. A. "The 'Twice-Born' Artists' Silent Revolution," *Black World* (May, 1971), pp. 58–67.

RANDALL, DUDLEY. "Portrait of the Poet as Raconteur," *Negro Digest,* XV, 3 (January, 1966), 54–57. Feature article gives insight into Tolson as philosopher, poet, and man.

Review, Anon., Los Angeles *Times,* n.d., quoted in "Wiley English

Professor Writes Best Seller," Wiley (Marshall, Texas) *Reporter,* May, 1945. Review of *Rendezvous with America* among Tolson's unpublished papers collected by Mrs. Ruth Tolson, Washington, D.C.

RICHARDSON, JACK. "The Black Arts," *The New York Review of Books,* XI, 2 (December 19, 1968), 10–13. Criticism of Black Consciousness Movement. Tolson is named as one of outstanding black writers in America.

"Rites Pending for Langston Poet-Teacher," *Daily Oklahoman,* August 30, 1966, p. 4. News story about death of Tolson.

RODMAN, SELDEN. "On Vistas Undreamt," New York *Times Book Review,* LIX, 4 (January 24, 1954), p. 10. Review of *Libretto.*

ROHRER, BOB. "Anderson Premiere Haunting," the Atlanta *Constitution,* May 27, 1970. Review of T. J. Anderson's "Variations on a Theme by M. B. Tolson."

SHAPIRO, KARL. "Decolonization of American Literature," *Wilson Library Bulletin* (June, 1965), pp. 843–54. Article attacks Establishment and names Tolson as one of three black poets whose poetry incorporates Negritude.

———. "Melvin B. Tolson, Poet," *Book Week,* New York *Herald Tribune,* January 10, 1965. Article published also as Introduction to *Harlem Gallery.*

SHERWOOD, JOHN. " 'Architect of Poetry': Harlem Poet's Epic Out 30 Years Later," the [Washington, D.C.] *Evening Star,* March 31, 1965, p. E–2, Review of *Harlem Gallery.*

SPECTOR, ROBERT DONALD. "The Poet's Voice in the Crowd," *Saturday Review* (August 7, 1965), p. 29. Review of *Harlem Gallery.*

"A Survey: Black Writers' Views on Literary Lions and Values," *Negro Digest,* XVII, 3 (January, 1968), 10–48, 84–89. Poll of black writers and critics reports their choices of outstanding black writers.

WHITE, CHAPPELL. "Anderson 'Variations' Shows Writer's Skill," the Atlanta *Journal,* May 27, 1970. Review of T. J. Anderson's "Variations on a Theme by M. B. Tolson."

3. Letters and Other Unpublished Written Commentary

CHAMBERLAIN, MARY LOU. Letter to M. B. Tolson, February 4, 1944. Editor for Dodd, Mead and Company invites Tolson to collect poems for book (*Rendezvous with America*). Letter with Tolson's unpublished papers collected by Mrs. Ruth Tolson, Washington, D.C.

CIARDI, JOHN. Letter to Richard L. Brown, assistant director, Bread

Loaf Writers' Conference, February 27, 1954. Recommends Tolson as Fellow at Bread Loaf Writers' Conference. Carbon copy sent to Tolson and now with his papers, Washington, D.C.

DILLON, GEORGE. Letter to M. B. Tolson, September 27, 1948. Letter from editor of *Poetry* magazine explains rejection of parts of *Libretto* for publication. Letter with Tolson's unpublished papers collected by Mrs. Ruth Tolson, Washington, D.C.

FLASCH, JOY. "Obsequies of Melvin Beaunorus Tolson, Senior," September 3, 1966. Gives insight into Tolson's contribution as poet, professor, and man (unpublished).

PERKINS, MAXWELL. Letter to M. B. Tolson, November 28, 1938. Explains rejection of "A Gallery of Harlem Portraits." Letter with Tolson's unpublished papers collected by Mrs. Ruth Tolson, Washington, D.C.

WADE, MARGARET WILLIAMS. Notebook consisting of lecture notes taken during English literature class taught by M. B. Tolson at Langston University, 1964–65. Reveals philosophical nature of poet-professor's lectures.

4. Interviews and Lectures

BONTEMPS, ARNA. Interview following Seminar, Negro History Week, Langston University, Langston, Oklahoma, February 12, 1969. Comment concerning Tolson's contribution to black America.

BROOKS, GWENDOLYN. Seminar, Negro History Week, Langston University, Langston, Oklahoma, Feburary 10, 1969. Comment on *Harlem Gallery.*

DICKEY, JAMES. Telelecture on Contemporary Literature originating from Stephens College, Columbia, Missouri, March 5, 1969. Evaluation of Tolson as a poet.

FARMER, JAMES. Commencement address, Langston University, Langston, Oklahoma, May 27, 1970. Comment about Tolson's influence on him as a student.

GOFF, JUANITA. Conversation, Langston University, Langston, Oklahoma, January, 1969. Former student of Tolson gives insight into his teaching methods.

JONES, WALTER. Conversation, Langston University, Langston, Oklahoma, December, 1968. Former colleague of Tolson gives insight into his philosophy and feeling about his life as he faced death.

OLIVER, CLINTON. "Definitive Qualities of Black Literature," Seminar, Black Heritage Week, Oklahoma State University, Stillwater, Oklahoma, February 13, 1969. Comments about Tolson as a black poet.

TOLSON, MELVIN B., JR. Conversations, 1965, 1966, 1967, 1968, 1970,

1971. Tolson's oldest son, Professor of Modern Languages, University of Oklahoma, Norman, Oklahoma, provided biographical information and assistance in interpreting passages in *Libretto* and *Harlem Gallery*.

TOLSON, RUTH. Conversations and letters, 1965, 1966, 1967, 1968, 1969, 1970, 1971. Widow of Melvin B. Tolson provided biographical information and insights into Tolson as poet and man. Made available his personal papers, which are now at her residence in Washington, D.C.

TOLSON, RUTH MARIE. Conversations and letters, 1967, 1968, 1969, 1970, 1971. Daughter of Melvin B. Tolson provided biographical information and assistance in going through his personal papers, which she has filed. Also assisted in finding secondary materials on Tolson.

WILSON, HELEN TOLSON. Conversation, August, 1967. Sister of Melvin B. Tolson provided biographical information about poet's early life and his parents and grandparents.

Index

(The works of Tolson are listed under his name)